SWIPE Write

A sometimes hilarious, sometimes sad, always brutally honest account of 20 online dates with 20 different men

LINDSAY TAYLOR DELLINGER

Published by Lindsay Taylor Dellinger, Los Angeles, CA

Printed in the United States of America

www.Lindsay-Taylor-Dellinger.com

Although the situations and scenarios in this book are largely as the author remembers them, some names and other identifying features and situations have been altered to protect privacy.

Contributing Editors: Amanda Gersh and Kasey Herrin

Book Design by Lindsay Taylor Dellinger and James Asuncion

Library of Congress Cataloging-in-Publication Data

Dellinger, Lindsay Taylor

Swipe Write – Revised ed.

LCCN 2021925110
ISBN 979-8-9854397-0-0 (paperback)
ISBN 979-8-9854397-1-7 (hardback)
ISBN 979-8-9854397-2-4 (eBook)

Subjects: Dating | Online Dating | Travel/Adventure | Love & Relationships [illegible] by Lindsay Taylor [illegible], Los Angeles, CA [illegible]

[illegible] in the United States of America

[illegible] Lindsay Taylor [illegible]lling.com

[illegible]

[illegible]

[illegible]

For my Mama, who always said: “She’s gonna be a writer someday.”

INTRODUCTION

I was once picked up in a grocery store during Mother's Day. "Excuse me?" a tall, bald Latino man interrupted my search for the perfect greeting card.

I turned toward him, my face flushing at the sight of his attractive, suit-clad appearance underneath the store's fluorescent lights. He smiled a charming and contagious, toothy grin. I wondered if he used Crest whitening strips. *Which aisle are those on*?

"I couldn't help but notice we were both on the hunt for Mother's Day cards. See anything good?" He asked.

It was the Friday before the holiday, so it was not entirely strange that two people were hunting for a card simultaneously, but I went with it.

"Not really, unfortunately," I told him.

"Would you like to have dinner tomorrow night?"

Wow, straight to the point. I liked that. I accepted his invitation.

This experience I had in my early twenties is probably a contributing factor as to why I was so anti-online dating. I realize my desire to meet the love of my life in the greeting card aisle of a grocery store while perusing Hallmark sentiments printed on glittered cardstock is somewhat prehistoric. I'm probably one of the last women in her mid-thirties shunning the idea of meeting someone online. Well, that and everyone knows the produce aisle is where it's at. One can tell a lot about a person's choice between romaine, kale, or iceberg.

Seriously, though, the dozens of people I knew for whom online dating was a less than subpar experience has also contributed to my anti-online dating attitude. Take the South African woman in her mid-sixties, for example, who nearly went on a date with a Nigerian scam artist she met online. Thank goodness her daughter intervened. Or how about the middle-aged businesswoman who went out with a man who divorced his wife because he'd watched her give birth to their child? He claimed he couldn't possibly look at her the same way anymore. *What in the actual fuck*?

The negative, downright appalling experiences seemed to outweigh the positive ones. I suppose the same could be said for any sort of dating. Still, I wondered, why complicate my life, any more than it already was, with online apps and potential danger? After all, I could meet a sleazebag at a bar during a girl's night out.

There were, admittedly, pros to the whole online dating thing. One of them is that you meet people that you'd otherwise probably never meet. I work in the fashion industry as an art director, primarily with apparel and product featuring a very famous Mouse, so it's never been difficult to meet other artists or creatives. Of course, unless I'm actively seeking the services of a lawyer, accountant, doctor, or related, it's doubtful we'll cross paths. Still, the number of Disneyland annual pass holders I know is grossly expensive!

"You have to go on at least twenty dates before throwing in the towel." My hairdresser insisted. Twenty was the number she threw out when I discussed my less than enthusiastic attitude toward continuing online dating.

"*With twenty different men*?!" I questioned with a shocked expression we could both see in the salon mirror.

"Yep," she responded.

Considering she had the outcome of my hair color *literally* in the palm of her hand, I complied. Challenge accepted. Coffee meets Bagel, a free dating app that three Korean sisters started, had a new client that night.

You're about to read a tale of twenty online dates, the others I met along the way, and what it means to search for love between emojis and overused acronyms. You're about to discover how an idealist with a less than subpar romantic track record navigated the modern dating world. While some of these encounters never quite make it past the pixels on my Smartphone screen, others pave the way for potential and self-growth.

Although things didn't pan out with my bald, Latino Mother's-Day-card-hunting man, I still romanticized meeting my future forever "organically." But, no, I didn't grow up dressing like Cinderella, waiting for my Prince Charming to bring me the glass slipper.

Hardly! In fact, in a nutshell, I'm a thirty-three-year-old, divorced, creative professional who never dreamt of getting married in the first place. No, that is not how my dating profile reads.

Here's how it reads, followed by my profile photos:

33, Los Angeles
Art Director, Private
FIDM

I am...
free-spirited, communicative, passionate, strong, open-minded, and creative. I'm also a pescetarian. I don't eat land animals but I love seafood! I'm excited about life - never bored. The word doesn't belong in my vocabulary.

I like...
Travel, yoga, writing, wine, hiking, animals, music, Hugs, sincerity, keeping it real

I appreciate when my date...
It's the little things that matter the most. A great sense of humor is always welcome.

Height
5' 3"

Education
FIDM/Bachelors
Fashion Institute of Design and Merchandising

Religion
Spiritual but not religious

Ethnicity
Other

Ice Breakers
I moved to Los Angeles when I was eighteen, two months out of high school. I knew no one and had never been here before.
I have misophonia
I enjoy traveling solo to far away destinations

And here's how it should have read: If you're going to fuck a writer, fall in love with a writer, or in many of the following cases, fuck *with* a writer, expect to be written about. And if you want nice things and sweet stories written about you, you should behave accordingly. The good news is, I'll always change your name. You're welcome. This is a self-approved public service announcement, AKA personal philosophy that I probably paraphrased from hours of scrolling through inspiring Pinterest quotes behind tear-filled eyes while sitting on the toilet.

*

My best friend, Norma, joined the encourage-Lindsay-to-try-online-dating bandwagon.

"Just see what's out there," She'd suggest, well maybe pressured a bit, but sometimes we need to be pressured into things we'd otherwise be closed off to. Her intentions were good. One night, while buzzed on sangria amid a busy bar in Studio City, teeming with inebriated albeit attractive men, she began the coercion.

It should also be mentioned that as we exited the bar, she unexpectedly played the world's greatest wing woman, telling an incredibly tall, dark, and handsome gentleman that her friend (yours truly) was attracted to him.

"I'm flattered, really, but I have a girlfriend." He politely informed her.

This should have been the beginning of a bolder, more adventurous me had I not run several feet ahead and hid in the dark shadows of a dirty stairwell.

By the time I got home from our exciting night of swiping left and right, I had my first online date scheduled for the following Saturday evening. My first impression of online dating was akin to sensory overload, and it could have gone on for as long as the app would allow me. It was like job searching; only the positions in my field were abundant. I couldn't believe I was doing this! I couldn't believe I even *had* a dating profile!

This is the part where I have to make sure you read the synopsis of this book. Everything henceforth is not PG; It's not even PG-13. It's rated R, or quite possibly whatever is beyond R. Hereafter, explicit language, descriptive scenes of nudity and sexuality, extreme crassness, and heavy sarcasm are prevalent. Got it? Great, let's continue.

YOU CAN SLEEP ON THE COUCH

Pro Dating Tip: A green thumb isn't always a green light.

His name was (*Insert basic, one-syllable, male name here*). He was a young surgeon, which is why we'll call him The Doctor. The Doctor was fit, in his mid-thirties, forearm veins visible, and he had the kind of lips that begged me to stare at them for a couple of seconds too long. He was going to pop my online dating cherry. In the week leading up to our date, we texted one another throughout the day.

One afternoon, he asked:

So, what are you looking for?

A genuine connection with someone I could potentially spend more time with. What are you looking for?

Hopefully, something serious.

We exchanged Instagram profiles during that week. I wasn't sure how I felt about that, and maybe this makes me sound antiquated, but I came from the last generation before cell phones became necessary.

There was no such thing as an "app" for most of my youth. Nonetheless, I liked what I saw: photos of his adoring parents and their outings to art museums and snapshots of his healthy plants boasting his green thumb. What more could a lady ask for? Okay, I can hear some of the skeptics rolling their eyes into the back of their heads, and I don't blame you. I'm sure my inner skeptic was off in a corner somewhere, snickering, pinky out as she sipped her red wine while I Instagram stalked him. Like, where were his friends? Surely his social life extended beyond immediate family? Maybe he had an entirely different Instagram handle altogether, and this was just the one he used for online dating?

The Doctor and I met on a Saturday night in downtown LA's Little Tokyo district at a sexy little bar named Baldoria. He initially wanted me to meet him at his downtown LA condo, but I declined the offer. I had to establish a set of rules for this whole online dating thing, and one of those rules was always to meet at the destination on the first date. This way, I have my own transportation should I need to hightail my ass out of there. And speaking of ass, The Doctor possessed a nice derriere. Of course, I wasn't just looking for external, temporary appeal, but a grab-worthy ass never hurt anyone.

He was standing outside the bar waiting for me, scoring him major points. It has always been about the little things in life for me and his waiting outside was a small gesture that went a long way. He hugged me upon our greeting, and that's when I noticed the solid physique underneath his sky-blue, collared shirt. He held the door open, and we went inside to take a seat at the bar, where he pulled out the stool for me. Well-dressed, excellent physical health, *and* chivalrous. Score!

The Doctor and I conversed about our favorite television shows and how we never had time to watch them. Our adoration for zombies and good sushi came up on more than one occasion, and thankfully we were on our way to having sushi for dinner. At one point, the half Japanese, half Chinese gentleman joked that I was more Asian than him after finding out I had a rice cooker at home while he didn't. Sense of humor? Check!

We dove right into religion and politics. He shared that he once ended a date with someone after she told him she'd voted for Trump. A man with conviction – *hot*.

The amount of flirting was just right, and we shared many a laugh throughout the evening. But, in what world was I living? It definitely wasn't the world that used to warn me about the dangers of meeting people online or downright forbid it. I intended to enjoy this gentleman's company for as long as it would last.

"What's your favorite color?" he asked as we walked a block to the sushi restaurant.

"Red."

"Passionate, aggressive, and knows what she wants." He quipped.

"You have me all figured out in less than an hour. Guess we can skip dinner and go home," I joked back.

After dinner, we had drinks at a barcade. As we were walking up to order, The Doctor placed his, for all I knew, insured hand on the small of my back. He was a surgeon, after all! Nonetheless, an attractive male's hand on the small of my back equals shockwaves down to my toes after making a detour at my lady parts.

He ordered the Moscow mule at our final destination, The Golden Gopher, a classic downtown LA hotspot. I questioned his alcoholic beverage of choice, being that he'd been drinking whiskey the entire evening. He told me he always orders the Moscow mule because, for every one sold, the bar donates to homeless causes. Had we not been in the middle of a bustling bar on a Saturday night, I would have blown him right there while he enjoyed his charitable adult beverage.

We found a cozy, dark corner to continue our titillating chat, at this point quite tipsy. As my head hung low, staring at the remainder of my wine swishing around in the glass, our conversation teetered between historic Japanese concentration camps in the middle of the California desert and his admirable, intimidating profession. His fingers found my hair, gently pushing it behind my ear. Again, with the small things – *my hair*. My hair is my strongest erogenous zone. One can pretty much get anything he wants by playing with my hair. That is if I don't fall asleep first.

I looked up to meet his seductive gesture, and instead, I met his sensuous lips. It was a very nice and welcomed first kiss. That's one of the more PG descriptions in this entire book. So earmark this page if you ever find yourself uncomfortable, and remember I have my moments. But also, we discussed this. The rest is not for the faint of heart, the squeamish, or the sensitive to language or blatant, intentional crassness.

Not long after our first kiss, we decided to Uber back to my car so that I could drive him the few blocks home.

"You have a Mazda 2?" He asked as we approached my car.

"No, it's a 3."

He meant, "Mazda, too," as in he also drove a Mazda. (*Insert tilted laughing/crying face emoji here*), which is probably what I looked like when I realized my mistake.

During the short drive to his place, he suggested I stay the night so that I didn't have to make the long drive home. Aww, how thoughtful, I did *not* think to myself. I knew what game he was playing, and I wanted to play, too.

"You can sleep on the couch. I won't touch you," he said as if that was some sort of incentive. I wanted him to touch me. I wanted to stay the night. I wanted more of his tongue in my mouth. I wanted to feel the skin underneath his button-down shirt. I wanted to run my fingers through *his* dark brown hair while his full lips found other parts of my hot and bothered body.

A mere ten minutes later, I was standing barefoot in his kitchen with a much-needed glass of water in my hand, admiring his corner condo's floor-to-ceiling windows overlooking downtown LA. I felt his arms slide around my waist from behind and the welcomed sensation of warm lips on the back of my neck (another thing that can pretty much get any man what he wants from me – neck kisses). That's not all it takes, though. Intellectual stimulation is a must, and that conversation must exceed the boundaries of our favorite fucking colors. Fortunately, ours had.

I felt him rise to the occasion through our jeans. I slowly turned my body toward his, our lips meeting again. I unbuttoned his shirt and felt his smooth, hairless skin with my fingertips before his mouth met my bare chest. We fucked on the first date, and against my better judgment, I spent the night.

The following morning was awkward as I woke prematurely, lying there listening to the low purr of The Doctor's snore. Would it be appropriate for me to get up and leave without waking him? Can I just wake him up and tell him I'm going? What are the rules for this type of situation? Before I figured it out, he woke up.

"You can't sleep?" He asked.

How did he know?

"Not really. I've been awake for a while."

At that point, I figured we'd get up, and I could leave, but he fell back asleep! Finally, after much tossing and turning, and about an hour later, he couldn't escape the disturbance that was a semi-stranger in his bed.

"I need to get home to feed my cats." That wasn't a lie.

He walked me to my car.

"I had a great night, and I'm looking forward to seeing you again," he stated.

"Likewise." I smiled.

We hugged, bidding one other a good day.

On the ride home, the night's activities replayed in my sober mind. So, the Doctor loved toes, specifically in his mouth? Is that considered a foot fetish? I asked Google, but they only gave me some mumbo jumbo about an Internet study group where 33% of 5,000 people had a fetish related to body weight or feet. (*Insert inquisitive, thinking emoji here*).

I have to admit, this was a first for me, and I didn't necessarily dislike it. Had it not been for the alcohol happily swimming in my veins, I may have been more self-conscious. However, it certainly added to the maintenance of my dating beauty regimen:

- Freshly laundered socks
- Callouses and rough heels banished
- Double the number of pedicures

In summation, it's pretty expensive dating a man with a hands-on, er, tongue-on liking to toes.

It became quickly apparent that The Doctor's greatest dating weapon of defense was his chosen profession. What better excuse to cancel plans than being called to perform emergency surgery? So, after the third date, in which we didn't fuck, I wasn't necessarily ghosted, but I was what I like to deem "back-pocketed."* I was placed on the backburner in case my grass became greener than the garden he was watering.

Remember how I said The Doctor and I followed each other on Instagram? Yeah? Well, it didn't take me long to notice the other women he began following during our three-month interim when his work was so overwhelming and time-consuming for his dating life. (*Insert eye-rolling emoji here*). Maybe emergency surgery was code for a hot date? He had a type, too. I was "it" minus the mask of makeup and body-con wardrobe.

"Are you even interested anymore? Because I'm not trying to waste my time or yours," I asked him after two weeks had gone by and there'd been no attempt at another date.

We were speaking on the telephone, mind you. I like to give people the benefit of the doubt. Most people deserve that. I also thought I'd better decipher the answer to my question through voice rather than text.

---

*My goal here is to create a hashtag for this bullshit - #backpocketed.

He claimed he was still interested and made one more failed attempt at setting up a date with me a few days later. Unfortunately, he canceled the day before due to, you guessed it, an "emergency surgery." *Benefit of the Doubt* may be Queen, but *Hindsight* is one royal bitch with perfect vision.

I couldn't be mad, though, right? The man improved people's overall quality of living. He was possibly saving someone's life or sucking on someone else's toes. But he'd had my toes in his mouth, his bodily fluids in my mouth, and his dick in my vagina! I think the least he could do was be upfront about whether or not he wanted to pursue anything further. Am I right, or *am I right*?

I'll make it up to you.

If a random text message here and there for two weeks was his idea of making it up to me, I didn't have any interest in finding out what other less than half-ass ways in which he conducted his intimate relationships. I wasn't going to put my life on hold for him or discontinue seeing what kinds of Bagels were available for the toasting.

SOAP OPERAS

When my third-grade teacher suggested to my mother that I was probably too young to be watching Susan Lucci's character, Erica Kane, strip down to her skivvies with just about every male character on the ABC soap opera, *All My Children*, she was probably right. Although, my mama didn't have it, and I don't blame her. Not only was another adult woman telling her that allowing me to watch such smut was lousy parenting, but those hour-long episodes also served as serious bonding time for her and me.

I would later repeat the drama with my dolls. Barbie and Ken's relationship was a lot like our favorite soap opera, only *ten times more* dramatic. Ken always ended up without a limb or two after being caught shacking up with one of Barbie's attractive, disproportionate friends. *Christie, how could you?* Sometimes Barbie would run Ken over with her three-wheeled pink convertible, or there would be an all-out domestic brawl. The scenarios were endlessly entertaining! No one ever came back from the dead, though, because I always scoffed at daytime drama's tendency to blur the credibility lines with that unbelievable situation.

"Don't ever settle," was something my mother repeatedly advised, having settled herself with my dad.

My father was a charismatic creature among perfect strangers while closing himself off to those who loved him the most. I was often left wondering what demons he was battling? How could I get through, make him see that he wasn't alone, that he was loved? I don't think these were questions I was asking myself at the age of fifteen when I first found out about his drug addiction, but they were undoubtedly questions I asked myself, at twenty-seven, when I married David, a man who mirrored my father on so many levels. Women often choose a mate uncannily similar to their fathers or so goes the adage.

"Men suck, and all the good ones are either gay or taken." My mom stated on more than one occasion during my childhood.

Mama was justified in her school of thought, and this idea was all but drilled into my skull. Yet, somehow, I continued to believe, maybe hope, that a good man did exist. I was determined not to settle until I found him while my mother spent almost twenty-five years trying to make it work with my dad.

Both of my parents passed away in 2011, four months apart. I was twenty-six years old. It was devastating, to say the absolute least. And, although my dad was gone, I still managed to make not so sound decisions when it came to the men I chose to give my time and energy to. So far, mom was right. Men did suck.

Even in acknowledging my tendency to choose not so well, I'm still human. And like any living, breathing human being, I wanted love, too. I'm more Erica Kane and Jackson Montgomery than Beauty and the Beast, though. This is probably due to my growing up fast, watching soap operas since the age of four, and having to call Grandma to fetch us during my dad's multiple drug binges.

THE WHITE ELEPHANT IN THE ROOM

Pro Dating Tip: Well-dressed doesn't always equate to being well-mannered.

Having grown up in India, the Lawyer was no stranger to large mammals. On a Thursday night in North Hollywood, I met him, online date #2. We'd met on Bumble, a dating app where the woman is required to make the first move.

I liked how well-traveled this man appeared to be. Although he worked in law, his interest in the arts was appealing, and, of course, I was physically attracted. He was very good-looking in a stuffed shirt kind of way, which left me wondering if there were any tattoos underneath that John Varvatos two-piece? His intense, dark eyebrows spoke more volume than his shampoo, and his green eyes seemed to sparkle every time he laughed.

"I watched elephants walk through my front yard regularly." He told me.

"I once saw a random duck waltzing its flat-footed feathery ass through my Midwestern American front yard."

We continued trading laughs. The night was going well.

Over a delicious malbec and Tuesday night jazz beats from the house band, I had a feeling I wasn't in Kansas anymore.

After two glasses of wine, The Lawyer glanced at his watch during our ongoing, lively conversation before anxiously jumping up.

"I gotta go!" He abruptly announced.

Before I could gather coherent thoughts, he was smoothing out his charcoal sport coat and turned toward the exit. I felt rushed while citing, "Yeah, I should get going, as well."

In less than two minutes, I was hugging him goodbye like two platonic strangers underneath The Federal Noho's neon-lit marquee and getting behind the wheel of my car. The abruptness in which he ended our date turned me off, though not enough to stop me from texting him, "Had a nice time" the following day.

He reciprocated the cordial sentiment, but I couldn't possibly know what prevented him from ever asking me out again. Whatever it was, it doesn't prevent him from following me on Instagram to this day. I stopped following him, for the record, although not before noticing he seemed happily engaged in another relationship with a lovely-looking lady. Maybe they met on Bumble! Either way, I should have stayed home and adopted an elephant for as much as we collectively spent on wine that night.

THE TYPHOON

The roar from the oncoming train at Tokyo's Shinjuku district excited all my senses. As I approached the platform, I reached out to The Doctor for the last time. The exchange was so brief and full of small talk. No more chasing anyone. That was another rule I'd set for myself upon embarking on this search for something real and unfamiliar.

Jet lag had me up at three 'o'clock in the morning, the first full day of my solo trip to Japan. So, I decided to walk the three miles to Gotokuji Temple, also known as the temple of the lucky cat, from my capsule hotel. If you don't know what a capsule hotel is, you must Google it *now*.

I wanted to pay homage to my beloved fur babies who passed away days apart from each other less than a month before I left for Japan. The first one, my youngest cat, died after a veterinarian unknowingly tore a hole in his trachea while inserting the intubation tube during routine dental cleaning. My oldest cat died ten days later due to unknown causes. I believe it was a broken heart. He'd been with me through every single thing that impacted my life, beautiful and tragic. He'd moved across the country with me, not once but twice, and was always there when I lifted my head up from any tearful moment. His eyes always said, "Don't cry, mama, I'm here."

I walked to the temple because I believe that on foot is the best way to see and get to know a city. After getting slightly lost and warmly greeted by an elderly Japanese woman standing in her front yard, I found the temple tucked away in a quiet neighborhood, shrouded by dewy hedges and cloudy morning light. I lit two pieces of incense, one for each of my fur boys, and said a silent prayer under the towering pine trees.

The temple was tranquil. There weren't very many visitors at 6 a.m., and a few men were unloading a truck full of cement blocks. I sauntered around in the solitude, stopping to read some of the ema. On these small, wooden plaques, temple goers write prayers or wishes. One, in particular, written by a Lindsey in the United States, caught my eye. The message was a wish for her two cats that had passed. It felt like a familiar reminder.

"I'm here, mama."

I walked to an area with hundreds of beckoning cats greeting me with their flapping, little plastic, porcelain, and wooden arms. A young woman was taking professional photos of the feline objects waving their limbs up and down, up and down. We made eye contact, exchanging a polite smile.

I didn't feel comfortable assuming she spoke English, but this tourist took the chance and said, "Hello." I quickly learned this was her second trip to Japan, and she was doing it solo this time. Her first trip was with her father. I wondered what it would have been like to travel such distances with my father? The closest I'd come was when he drove me halfway across the country from Kansas City to Los Angeles two months after graduating high school. My mother threatened to kill him if he took pills while making the trek with me. And he didn't, take pills that is, until his solo return trip.

The friendly American from San Diego brought two handmade, painted cats to add to the temple's giant collection. After some small chat, we exchanged numbers. Our travel plans had us crossing paths in Kyoto a few days later, where we decided we'd meet for dinner.

On my second and last night in Tokyo, I met with two essential strangers. The woman, Mikari, had worked with one of my best friends stateside years prior. Mikari was originally from Japan and had moved back. She brought her boyfriend to show me around Tokyo. Up until that moment, we'd been conversing through Whatsapp, a free messaging service owned by Facebook.

This really wasn't much different than online dating when I thought about it. I wasn't completely sold on the whole online dating thing just yet. Still, if I could meet up with strangers solo in another country, I could definitely do this in my own home base.

The evening, despite my being exhausted, was incredible. I ate some of the best food I've ever had in my life (much of it, I wasn't even sure what it was). I was getting to experience the quintessential

Japanese culture from a local's perspective. We spent most of the day and night in Tokyo's Asakusa district, which has maintained much of the charm and wonder of an older Tokyo. After being taught how to do a Buddhist prayer at Tokyo's oldest temple, we dined at a street food stall where everyone around me was sitting so close together; it brought on a whole new meaning to "rubbing elbows." It was loud, and everyone was smoking cigarettes. This smoky, overcrowded environment would typically bother me, but I loved every second of it! My concerned tour guides graciously asked if I was okay with the secondhand smoke. I explained that I wanted the complete immersion into how they would be spending their evening if they weren't showing an American around.

As we bid our goodbyes and after expressing my thank-you's, Mikari's boyfriend, who didn't speak much English, insisted that I take his umbrella to prepare for the inevitable rain from the season's typhoons. I'd read up on Japanese culture "dos and don'ts," and remembering it's considered an insult to refuse a gift, I accepted.

The following day, I got off of a bus at the wrong stop when the typhoon made landfall in the town of Hakone, west of Tokyo. I was exceptionally grateful for that umbrella! I hopped on the next bus praying it was going the way I needed it. I finally made it back to my hostel, drenched from the downpour.

I retired my rain-soiled Pumas that night, thankful to Mikari's boyfriend, who insisted I take his umbrella. I showered and got into dry, comfortable clothes as I knew I'd be spending the evening indoors, in the comfort of my accommodations. Unfortunately, the rain was not letting up, and it was still so early. Luckily for me, the hostel had a bar. I took my travel journal with me, ordered a beer and a pizza, which was surprisingly halfway decent, and I sat at the bar writing.

Between sips of a beer as large as my head and journaling the day's adventures, a man walked into the hostel, looking as drenched and as exhausted as I had a couple hours earlier. I discreetly watched him check in and make his way upstairs to his room, hoping he'd come back downstairs, as thirsty and as hungry as I was. I was primarily thirsty for human interaction. If the human interaction came from an attractive male, this was a welcomed and added perk.

The early twenty-something female bartender from Australia had tired of me, resorting to conversing loudly with a coworker when much to my excitement, the weary male traveler emerged thirty minutes later, his brown hair still damp from showering. With plenty of empty seats at the bar, he chose to sit right next to me.

As he deliberated on what to order, I recommended the pizza. This resulted in a delightful, almost two-hour conversation. I learned that this late twenties Canadian man named Eric with the wavy, disheveled hair lived in London and worked in finance. He frequently traveled solo. We realized our itinerary was the exact opposite, he had just arrived from Kyoto, which was where I was headed, and I had just come from Tokyo, which was where he was headed.

Eric was interesting, albeit slightly guarded. I didn't get him to divulge too many personal details. There was definitely something that urged this gentleman to travel alone. That much, I could gather. A broken heart, I presumed.

He told me all about the onsen* that I needed to try at least once before leaving Hakone. This particular one was first-come, first-served, and, surprisingly, not gender-segregated. I'd also been looking forward to relaxing in an onsen before I left Japan.

After connecting via Instagram, we said our farewells and I made my way to the, thankfully, unoccupied onsen. While enjoying the unique experience, Eric was messaging me from his room asking if I'd made it or if someone else beat me to it. I almost asked if he'd like to join me and instead chose to enjoy the first-time experience all by myself.

I think back and wonder if it was loneliness or just freedom that urged me to invite this man to bathe with me? I think it was mainly freedom, having the control to do as I pleased. No one was looking

---

*An onsen is a Japanese hot spring heated by a nearby volcano. They can be found all over Japan, and most are gender-segregated because one must be nude while bathing.

for me. I was in a foreign country, and if I wanted to have a one-night stand with a Canadian solo traveler I'd just had a beer and good conversation with, then I was going to. Hell, if I only wanted to skinny dip with a stranger, then so be it!

I contemplated asking if he'd like to come to my room afterward. I was sincerely enjoying his company. One of the joys of traveling solo is meeting other solo travelers and exchanging stories of adventures. If there was no other connection, there was always travel. And at the end of the day, every human craves and needs connection. In all honesty, I think I didn't extend the invitation because I was getting up before dawn to catch the train to Osaka. I needed some shut-eye.

The following morning, I awoke early as planned. It was so early the sun hadn't even reached that side of the hemisphere. I left the umbrella with a note by the entrance to the hostel in the hopes that it would come in handy for someone else the way it had come to my rescue - a sort of pay-it-forward if you will. Making my way on foot to the train station with thoughts of Eric in the back of my mind, wishing him well and an enjoyable remainder of his solo excursion.

I believe in that, you know? Call it sending positive vibes or putting out positive energy. Call it whatever you want. I suppose you could even venture to call it prayers, but *I believe in it*. I think it somehow gets back to that person in a positive way, just like negative thoughts and attitudes can permeate a situation or someone's day.

Have you ever woke up feeling like shit and believing that everything is shit and then everything about your day is shit? Yeah, that's what I mean.

Waiting for the train to arrive, a beautiful, shorthaired calico cat went darting across the platform in a blur of cream, terracotta, and chocolate, disappearing into the bushes. It wasn't the last time I'd experience an encounter with a cat while traveling in Japan. Some might argue how easy those encounters come as there are a plethora of stray cats all over that country. I took it as a message from my babies, though. They were there, somewhere, wishing *me* well.

The train ride was enjoyable. I love sunsets and that mesmerizing golden hour, but there's something exceptionally magical about the dawn and its sunrise. I saw the sunrise almost every single day I was in Japan because of the jet lag. It was truly extraordinary - a sobering reminder that another day had commenced. We all had another opportunity to do something we may have feared the day before, another chance to start over, to find which we seek, and another chance to *connect*.

FAIRYTALES

I bumped into the man who would become my husband, David, one year after our initial meeting at the same Mexican restaurant in Manhattan's lower west side. We decided to spend the following four days together: That meant breakfast, lunch, and dinner, sleep, repeat. He eventually professed his love for me on my last night in New York City, on a rooftop in Midtown. I don't know if someone can sincerely fall in love in ninety-six hours, but the feelings were mutual even though it took me a while to reciprocate the words.

Our relationship began long distance, him in New York City and me in Los Angeles until I made the cross-country move closing the two thousand plus mile gap. I thought I'd met the one; the one who I didn't feel like I was settling for and the one who was everything my mother didn't believe existed.

I cited the whole "It's just a piece of paper" argument every time he brought up the prospect of marriage. I eventually agreed to marry him because he grew up Catholic and delivered a very moving, compelling speech about all the reasons why marrying me was so important to him. He also delivered this speech naked, on bended knee in an MGM Grand hotel room in Las Vegas. Two years after, to the day we met, we tied the knot in New York City's downtown courthouse surrounded by his immediate family, my older brother, and our closest friends. ~~And we lived happily ever after!~~

The beginning and plot of our story were better than a fairytale. Cinderella had nothing on that shit! Who willingly wears fucking glass slippers anyways? I wasn't looking for fairytales, however. *Remember*? I grew up on daytime dramas. I was looking for my ride or die.

The thing that no one tells you when you're four years old is that somewhere in between Disney princess films and "happily ever after" lies all of the ick – the human complexities, the grey areas, and the external, contributing factors toward our tendency to choose unwisely. These not-so-cute learned behaviors make relationships of any kind seem less than perfect.

ほとんどありません HOTONDO ARIMASEN & I LIKE TO FEEL

Upon exiting the train to catch my connection to Nara, a train employee also stepped off the train further down the platform. Standing in his neatly pressed navy uniform, he began vigorously waving in my direction, his gloved hand a haze of white above his conductor's hat. Does he think he knows me?

Of course, I waved back because that's the polite thing to do, though I should have looked behind me first. Another train employee was at the opposite end of the platform, enthusiastically returning this man's greeting because they, in fact, did know one another. I turned back toward my new friend, embarrassment engulfing my face in a hot flash, and he bowed to me several times, this time his hands placed in prayer as we shared a giggle at my mistake.

Nara, Japan's fall landscape was dotted with a plethora of wild deer, the greenest grass, and pristinely manicured gardens that looked like they'd just waltzed out of some fairytale. It was my fifth day in Japan, and I found myself staring at the most majestic scene I'd ever witnessed to date, Nara Park.

Standing alone, basking in the early morning sun, I thought about how I wished I could share the moment with a significant someone.

I wanted someone to be witnessing this natural beauty at the same time as I was. That's not to say I wasn't grateful to be witnessing such splendor solo. Enjoying the mystical glory that I was the only human being in that exact place at that exact moment on this vast Earth was definitely something to write home about. I like to have faith that during those times when I'm having those transcending thoughts, in some way, great or small, I'm manifesting what is to come. And if I'm feeling particularly jaded that day, I tell the endless, innate hope inside of me to *fuck off*.

Nara was a dreamscape. The history was palpable, the food incredible, and the feelings overwhelming. I only spent a few hours there and somehow managed to find myself in a deluge of emotion on two separate occasions. I'm not just talking about a half-assed tear or two. I'm talking full-on, uncontrollable sobbing at places for memorials and peace.

Instead of finding someone to watch my cats while I was overseas, I made space on an antique coffee table for their ashes and paw imprints. It was the same table that once served as my family's dinner table under which I once hid from my dad's drug-induced rage. Their casts were placed right next to photos of other family members who I'd lost over the years, including my parents. It was my own personal shrine.

The tears I was shedding in Nara weren't just out of grief for the losses I've endured throughout my life. They were also tears of gratitude for my health and my ability to travel. I finally felt like I'd made it, and I'd done so primarily on my own. Something otherworldly was also comforting me, an intense knowing that my parents would be proud of me, especially my mother.

I had some time to kill before my train arrived to take me from Nara to Kyoto that afternoon. So I walked around the city streets, stumbling upon a shrine that doubled as a cemetery. It was built into an unassuming block surrounded by high rises and noisy traffic though it still managed to present a sense of calm. I walked up the shallow steps while the high noon sunshine warmed my bare shoulders. Sitting down on a bench, I noticed I was the only one there, and I wept without warning. The tears just started falling, and I couldn't catch my breath.

In my peripheral vision, I noticed I was no longer alone. An old Japanese man with thin-wired glasses slowly walked up the steps. His hands were clutching one another behind his back. I discreetly tried stifling the tears and wiping my face. Shockingly, he was making his way toward me. His walk was full of so much intent that if I didn't know better, I would've believed his entire purpose of visiting that shrine was to see me. As he neared, he bowed. I returned the bow, still sitting. I was surprised at his close proximity, as the Japanese tend to be a culture of well-defined personal space. He spoke to me in Japanese, revealing several gold-capped teeth with a smile and kind eyes that never left mine. I returned a confused smile.

"I'm sorry, I don't speak Japanese. Do you speak any English?"

He smiled bigger and said something else in Japanese before bowing, turning, and walking into the building opposite the bench I was sitting on.

I felt light from him as he disappeared behind the wooden structure. I truly believed he was sent to me at that moment. Sure, we couldn't communicate with language, but his eyes and his expression said everything I needed to hear at a time where I was feeling utterly alone. *I wasn't alone*. And who knows, maybe I was also sent to him for some reason?

*

Ten months after David and I separated, I unexpectedly fell for someone at work who henceforth shall be called Anthony. Anthony didn't fit the description of what I'd come to think of as "my type" by any means. I think that was a part of the appeal.

I realize how much I don't really have a type as I age. I mean, sure, tall, dark, and handsome, but what sane woman doesn't like that? Have you ever heard a woman exclaim, "short, pale, and average," as what floats her boat? I don't think so. Truth is, though, not all of the men I've found myself attracted to fit the bill. I started noticing how varied my taste was becoming. It was actually quite thrilling that I'd reached a level of maturity dictated more by what was on the inside than a handsome exterior. Sure, I still needed to be physically attracted to the person, but allowing myself to go beyond looks gave me a strange sense of curiosity. I discovered what I already knew on a much deeper level – a great personality could make an average-looking human attractive. It also made me wonder how many connections are missed because someone is too shallow to see past a less than pretty face.

Anthony was a subdued, introverted artist, so suspicious of others that he'd leave pennies underneath his bedroom door when he knew maintenance was coming over to fix the leaky pipe in his kitchen. If the door wasn't covering the penny when he returned home, then that was proof that maintenance was going where they didn't belong. What he'd do with the "proof" remained to be seen, considering the door never moved.

While kind and giving, he allowed me to wear the pants too often in the relationship. I was the first person to walk up to a host in a restaurant, I made all the plans, I defended the both of us when necessary, thereby becoming anxious, exhausted, and bored.

"How come you never talk about our future? Don't you see yourself with me?" I asked him on several occasions.

"I don't talk about it because you're the one who always says you don't want to get married or have kids, so why would I?"

This conversation repeated itself for the nearly three years we invested in one another. I would tirelessly explain to Anthony that there is more than just marriage and kids in the future of a relationship. We could travel the world, cohabitate, and volunteer together – the possibilities were endless! If he wanted the former, though, I wanted to know that, too. I wanted to know when he was upset or angry, but I could rarely extract much emotion from him. Complacency was rampant in his world, and I was passionate, often deemed as confrontational.

"I think you like to fight." He once said to me.

That wasn't true at all.

"*I like to feel*," I corrected him.

I conducted my part in the relationship with the familiar mentality that if I loved enough, gave enough, and worked hard enough, then things would change. It took me a handful of years later to figure out that if I was ever going to find what I truly wanted and deserved, *I had to change*.

I needed to change the pattern of what I was attracted to, which began with the excitement of the unpredictable, outgoing narcissist. When that relationship became too venomous, I craved the calmness from the more passive personality of the artist, and, well, you get the picture. What all of these men had in common was their lack of emotional availability. And who did that unfailingly remind me of? My father. So unconscious was this pattern that I needed to figure out how to identify the signs before I got too far. I needed to begin healing.

This office love affair didn't end well. I'm sad to say I lost a great friend in the process, which was the most difficult part for me. But Erica Kane taught me that the best way to get over someone is to get under another, and The Doctor, if nothing else, was sexy temporary relief.

My first night in Japan happened to be Anthony's birthday. Of course, he was still on my mind, not to mention I'd asked him to come to Japan with me while we were still together. As he hesitated the way he'd hesitated with so much of our relationship, I reneged my offer.

"Never mind. I don't want you to come." I simply said.

And I meant it. I meant it the way The Doctor meant it when he got up and left his Trump-voting online date – *without a doubt and with conviction.* I didn't wallow in the rejection either. Since I'd ended things three months before my vacation, I couldn't think of a better way to begin that healing process, to start letting go, than vacationing in a foreign country.

Later that night, after my experience with the old man in Nara, I bathed until I became a prune in the bathroom of my hotel room in Kyoto. I wrote out the state of my feelings about my recent losses (my cats and now ex-boyfriend, Anthony), and I posted them to Instagram alongside a photo of that magnificent, mesmerizing deer-dotted dawn from Nara Park. What was happening inside of me, emotionally? What was happening spiritually?

LaChele, one of my closest friends, texted me that night:

Girl!

It was a four-letter word almost as powerful as love when exchanged between the two of us. She in Los Angeles and me in Southeast Asia, I felt relief in breaking my silence in the awkward sphere of social media. She was texting me to affirm my actions, to adorn my cell phone screen with virtual high fives and kissy face emojis.

There was a "letting go" of sorts that night in a tiny Japanese bathtub. I emphasize "Japanese" before bathtub because these things are truly something special. They're typically not the standard rectangular, porcelain ones you might be used to seeing or bathing in. They're small, deep, and if you've never seen or experienced one, Google Image it now.

The following evening, I met with Bryndan, the San Diegan woman I'd met at the cat temple. After a drink at a random French bar in the Gion neighborhood of Kyoto, we had dinner at a seafood restaurant near the iconic Kamo River. It was very easy to talk to her. Just as we'd connected so quickly in the early morning hours at a temple dedicated to cats, we casually shared intimate details of our lives over the fresh catch of the day.

By this time, my knee had begun giving out on me from all the walking in my heeled boots, so I wasn't planning to do much more walking after dinner. Instead, I took a taxi back to the hotel where I proudly told the driver that we were "almost there" in Japanese - with the help of Google Translate, of course.

"Hotondo arimasen!" I exclaimed.

I discovered much later that this is not the proper way to say it. Nonetheless, the taxi driver appreciated my effort with a jolly laugh and a thankful bow of his head.

I wondered if this were true, though. Was I almost there? And was passion of the pixelated kind all part of the journey?

WABI-SABI

I spent the next few days in a foreign land searching for human connection and crying some more, the release feeling surprisingly good. On my last night in Japan, I felt very pretty. It was the kind of pretty where you're having a good hair day, and your skin appears flawless. I wished I had someone to share the moment with once again. I lay on the traditional tatami mat floor of my hostel in the seaside town of Kamakura with tears flowing before deciding to saunter over to the beach. I admired the sunset's sorbet-colored sky playing catch me if you can with the Pacific and the many couples and families around me partaking in the same simple pleasure.

Afterward, I opted to drink all of my Japanese yen at a wine bar. I'd discovered the place was directly across the street from my hostel while planning my trip. Yes, that is part of why I booked my stay there. Some patrons were impressed by how much vino I could consume without becoming completely sloshed. As I drank delicious wines from all over the world, including Japan, the bartender said something in Japanese to the gentleman sitting a couple of seats to my left. His comment was instantly met with a shared, boisterous laugh that was obviously about me.

"What's so funny?" I blurted out.

To my surprise, the gentleman to my left spoke English.

"The bartender is impressed that you just drank an entire bottle of wine by yourself." He informed me.

"It's in my genes."

We shared a giggle. There were only about ten people in the tiny place, including the cook and the bartender. I did manage to drink all of my yen, and I prompted more laughs from the locals as I counted coins to settle my bill. I inadvertently discovered the cultural faux pas of paying with coins spans the globe!

Shortly after my blatant singledom was placed on blast through my love for vino, I retreated to my room, where I dropped my smartphone on my face before passing out cold. So much for that flawless skin. It had been a while since I'd had any real human contact – a hug, a touch – Hell, there wasn't even an accidental brush up against anyone because that's just how orderly and polite the Japanese are. Of course, this was also primarily due to the language barrier, and I'm actually grateful for this experience. I feel like it made me even more attuned to the importance of our relationships, no matter how significant or small.

On November 4th, 2017, my last night in Japan, I wrote in my journal: *When you're twenty-five years old, romance is a priority. We recklessly seek it, even if it means sacrificing our own needs. The older I get, the more I realize it doesn't have to be like that. In fact, if we're sacrificing our own needs for someone, chances are he/she isn't the right one.*

When you solo travel, you go to places of self-discovery that you've never gone to before. You leave pieces of yourself behind and take pieces of others as you continue your journey. In Japan, there's a form of art called Kintsugi, where cracked pottery is repaired with gold creating an aesthetically pleasing appearance. It's heavily influenced by the Japanese philosophy of wabi-sabi. Wabi-sabi invokes our ability to see the beauty in our flaws and accept imperfections. I began believing my heart had to be broken into pieces so that I could give them away to others who might need it, recalling the old man's gold-capped, toothy grin in Nara.

I arrived home quite late after my twelve-hour flight connection from Beijing. When I walked in the door, the warm, familiar, and furry friends I'd become so accustomed to in the past twelve years weren't there to greet me. The reminder of their untimely death plowed into me.

I decided masking my grief with the presence of testosterone was the best course of action for my jet-lagged brain. So I picked up the phone and sent a text message to a man I'd briefly dated in the interim when Anthony and I broke up and got back together. We'll call him AJ.

Earlier that year, I broke his heart by abruptly calling it off citing the, "It's not you, it's me" bullshit. I was actually giving round two with Anthony a go. In retrospect, I should have just been honest, but I suppose I need to accept my imperfections. Maybe there's some beauty to be found somewhere in my dishonesty? Or maybe I'm just an asshole.

AJ, too, was a cat lover, and he knew all too well what it was like to lose such close companions. He offered to keep me company. I was fortunate he even agreed to come over, but maybe we both needed each other that night. He spent the night. We cuddled. Our clothes stayed on. We kissed, and he left the following morning, kissing me again before I went to see my therapist for a much-needed session.

UNEXPECTED STATESIDE ENCOUNTERS

Pro ~~Dating~~ Life Tip: Try not to hit your date or anyone for that matter while searching for parking.

Whoa! he stepped out in front of my vehicle, doe-eyed and hands defensively lifted in the air. Only going about three miles per hour, I nearly hit my date with my car while searching for parking. We recognized each other at the same time. I rolled my window down and smiled as we shared a nervous laugh.

"Sorry about that! I'll be there shortly – just gotta park."

I was still recouping from jet lag upon my return from Japan when a coworker expressed her desire to set me up with a friend of hers. He was thinking about moving to California from New York City, and she felt she could help make his transition easier and/or more appealing with another friendly face. Mine.

While our introduction didn't begin on an online dating app, it did begin with technology. A few pleasantries and overly sarcastic text messages later, I debated whether or not I even wanted to give this stranger my valuable time. My concerns lay in his inability to take anything seriously through our initial exchange. Every other response was cynical, trite, and full of seemingly defensive quips.

Curiosity got the best of me, or maybe I was just looking for a challenge. Nonetheless, I agreed to meet him at a bar in Sherman Oaks on a Wednesday night.

Wow was my initial thought when we officially met in person. His towering stance required him to bend over to greet me with a hug. When he spoke, a hint of Spanish accent made my skin flush, especially when combined with his dizzying smile. His face was shaven, though the five-o-clock shadow showed even in the bar's dim lighting.

This Dominican Republic-born, tattoo-less Adam Levine look-alike was quick-witted, funny, passionate, intelligent, curious, and attentive with a smile that could make anyone, and I mean, anyone swoon – even the male, very straight bartender serving us our very adult beverages.

I was concerned about the entire evening being full of sarcasm, and while I do love sarcasm, I'm happy to report it was minimal. Our meeting consisted of a healthy balance between serious, sarcastic, and flirtatious. It was clear we were feeling each other, and I found myself thanking my aforementioned curiosity and my coworker.

We chatted about our love for travel and my recent trip to Japan. I told him about the gold-capped toothed man at the shrine.

"What do you think he was saying to you?" Mr. East Coast inquired.

It was a deep, great question that I was glad he asked.

"I like to believe he was telling me that everything's gonna be all right. He brought me so much hope and comfort in our twenty-second exchange. Those moments are few and far between, and I'll cherish and remember that man forever."

After a couple glasses of red vino, we walked out into the cool, November evening air, continuing our conversation. I turned to face him and give him a hug as his left hand grabbed the side of my face, fingers tracing the back of my neck. He pulled me in for a kiss. It was full of fervor and lasted long enough to render me self-conscious of the PDA. I lost my breath, and if it weren't for his other hand around my waist, I might have stumbled into the brick wall behind me.

"I'm going to see you tomorrow." Mr. East Coast said with that sexy, subtle accent after releasing my lips from his.

It was not in the form of a question. It was unmistakably, *unequivocally* a statement.

And I did – *see him tomorrow,* that is.

The following evening, he came to my place, where we sat on my living room floor after I poured a couple glasses of wine.

"Come closer," He commanded playfully with a seductive leer.

I inched a little closer. With his forefinger, he motioned for me to come even closer, casually tilting his head while doing so and baring that panty-dropping smile.

Again, I moved my body closer to his.

"Closer," He whispered, the heat escaping his mouth and landing on my exposed torso.

I draped my legs around his waist, straddling him while we both sat upright, our faces just inches away from the other. He leaned in. This time, it was I tilting my head as he kissed my neck ever so gently. He kissed my shoulder, inhaling sharply when his mouth met my ear before softly kissing my neck again. It felt like forever – sweet, stimulating torture I would welcome for eternity.

Our bodies found my bed. Our clothes found the carpeted floor, and our naked bodies found each other. After we had sex, we lay in bed, our arms wrapped around one another. We were consumed in literal pillow talk while philosophizing about the human experience. The comfort level was beyond any I've ever experienced with someone I'd only just met. Sensual and connected are the two words I use to describe that incredible night.

“How do you feel about me spending one more night with you, postponing my trip to San Francisco?” Mr. East Coast asked in the dark that had taken over my bedroom.

Wow, I thought. This man just met me, and he's already changing his plans for me. I'm not chasing him. I'm not asking him. Instead, he's asking me how I feel about him staying with me one more night - this time, in the form of a question but definitely not sans the personal desire.

Initially, I asked him if he'd be postponing something important. I didn't want to get in the way of such things. Realizing I just wasn't used to this behavior, I expressed that I wanted him to spend one more night with me because I did. His intentions were clear, and I also needed to make mine clear.

"I would like that very much," I finally told him, feeling triumphant in my ability to identify the unfamiliar.

The following day, a Friday, I went to work, and he explored more of LA before we met back at my place in the evening. We could barely keep our hands off of each other, but hunger got the best of us. I took him to one of my favorite Cuban spots, where we shared a plate of calamari before I dined on fish with their signature rice and beans and he, the pulled pork.

Mr. East Coast connected with our waiter, conversing in Spanish about where each of them was from and the delicious food we'd just consumed. I admired his friendliness and the sincerity that encompassed it. It was bold and curious, a delightful setting for a not-so delightful declaration.

"*I'm afraid of commitment.*" He dropped the bomb, the other shoe. It was the proverbial catch I always find myself waiting on when things seem too good to be true. "I know that's not what any self-respecting woman wants to hear," he hesitantly continued.

"Well, I'd rather hear the truth any day than what people assume I want to hear. At least you're honest."

I meant it while feeling a profound sting of disappointment. I don't know what I thought it could become because we lived on opposite coasts, but maybe there was a bit of personal fantasy at play. Somewhere in between Mr. East Coast changing his plans to spend more time with me and enjoying our first dinner together, I imagined he'd move to the west coast resulting in this palpable connection becoming more than just a memorable weekend.

On the ride home, Mr. East Coast asked to play a song on his mind. He chose a Spanish ditty by Luis Enrique. The song's name was "Yo No Se Mañana," which is basically about a man professing how he has no idea what tomorrow will bring, so he just wants to live for today. *Message received.*

That night, we made passionate love for the second time, and the condom broke.

"*I'm clean.* I was recently checked," he hastily assured, hovering over me in the heated aftermath of his climax. I assured him of the same as well as the added benefit that my tubes had been tied a year prior.

No worries – there won't be any mini-Mr. East Coasts running around in nine months, I thought to myself. Deciding to tie my tubes was an impulsive decision but not one that I regret by any means. On the contrary, I was definitely grateful for my impulsive decision when a condom broke with a man I'd only just met. And a man afraid of commitment, no less!

The following morning, I had to leave early for therapy, so we said goodbye as we sat on the edge of my bed. When we embraced, it was like hugging someone I'd known for years, not someone I'd only met a few days ago. All of the uncertainty of the future but the beauty and grace of a sincere connection swirled around our bodies. Our arms didn't want to release one another from that hug.

I could also feel the disenchantment from the night before settling in like a dense fog no one wants to drive in. No amount of foreplay, stimulating conversation, or Cuban food could make this man unafraid of commitment.

I'm very good at appearing "fine," however. Suffice it to say, I've become an all-out pro. I think, sometimes, some of us become so good at saving face and pretending to be "fine" that we actually begin to believe and fool ourselves until the energy it takes to do so becomes so depleted, there's nowhere else to go but the floor or the bottom of a wine bottle. I've been to both more times than I have fingers to count.

And yet, I didn't foresee myself ceasing to pursue his affections or deny his advances. Why? Because I'd never felt this kind of connection with anyone. It was more than sexual and certainly more than romantic. I truly cared for this soul and felt that he genuinely cared for me.

Later that night, I texted Mr. East Coast:

I can't help but let you know how sad I was to see you go this morning.

He returned my sentiment with a phone call as he drove his rental somewhere north between LA and San Francisco.

"I'm really grateful to have met you and spent these last few days with you," I told him.

"I feel the same way, LindsAy." Endearingly, he always emphasized the "A" in my name through voice and text.

I was in a strange limbo between an endorphin-induced high grounded by his announcement that, even if my fantasies were to play out and he was to move to Los Angeles, he was *afraid of commitment*. Even knowing that was just the sort of unavailability I needed to avoid, I wasn't sure I would. Mr. East Coast and I agreed to keep in touch while I didn't know if that would be enough for me. I decided I wasn't going to put my life on hold and stop online dating but I wasn't going to stop talking to him, either.

OH......MY......GOD

Pro Dating Tip: Keep in mind that sometimes, they'll remind you of someone...in the worst way.

I liked his no-beating-around-the-bush style. So even though I'm allergic to all kinds of anesthesia, I obliged when this anesthesiologist in his late thirties asked if I'd like to meet after a thirty-minute Coffee meets Bagel chat. It was a lazy Sunday afternoon when I met him for coffee and what would be my third official online date. We met at Romancing the Bean café in Burbank.

Surely you remember Janice from *Friends*? Yeah, I was on a date with Janice, only Janice was a man and I wasn't Chandler. Imagining Janice say "OMG" before my name, should we ever meet again, gave me more of an allergic reaction than any anesthesia I've ever been administered. Need I say more?

GOOGLE ISN'T ALWAYS RIGHT

Pro Dating Tip: Social media profiles should remain uncharted territory if you haven't completed a second date with someone you've met online.

Online date number four asked if we could meet near his apartment. A block away, to be precise. Not a great sign. One strike against him, and we hadn't even met. The thirty-something mental health therapist couldn't even make an effort to meet me halfway, which would have been the polite thing to do. Angelenos. If you know, you know.

Strike two was the profuse sweating. Sure, this wasn't his fault, but it was a definite turn-off. And strike three was Mr. Sweat's glaring "me, me, me" syndrome. His forehead glistened under the seedy bar's neon lights as he praised himself for being a good listener, which led to his choice of profession. *Ha*! I immediately felt terrible for his patients.

Why after three strikes, you might ask, did I still choose to take a walk to his apartment after a couple of adult beverages? I frankly had nothing better to do, and I didn't feel like being alone. If I knew something was never going to go beyond a flippant make-out session, there was absolutely no harm in enjoying a flippant make-out session. Whether I *enjoyed* said make-out session was TBD.

Had I said three strikes and I'm out, I wouldn't have the pleasure of telling you about the part where Mr. Sweat thought playing guitar and serenading me in his upper floor condo overlooking the downtown Los Angeles cityscape was going to make me want to sleep with him. I wouldn't be able to tell you that his bathroom was not clean or that my shirt came off and went back on shortly after his tongue grazed my tits.

After the music ended and the buzz wore off, I was ready to leave. I knew I never wanted to see him again. We had a cordial conversation, but there was no connection. Cordial is a nice way of describing an exchange one might have with her mailman; only, this date wasn't delivering anything except for some perspiration to my upper lip. (*Insert barfing emoji here*).

When Mr. Sweat hit me up for a second date a couple of days later, I asked Google, "How do you politely let an online date down?" Google informed me that a text message was acceptable, justifying the impersonal aspect of this form of communication because I didn't owe him anything. Google had spoken!

I texted him:

I really enjoyed your company the other night, but I don't see this going past anything platonic.

He was clearly hurt. His response was unfollowing me on Instagram. Of course, he shouldn't have started following me in the first place. We should all know what we're getting ourselves into when we agree to meet up with a total stranger through an application designed for our sometimes explosive, battery-operated handheld devices.

Sure, I was thoughtful in not ghosting Mr. Sweat, but I decided that Google was wrong. Some of these situations didn't even warrant a textplanation, and yes, I just made that word up.

MAKING PASTA IN A VAMPIRE DEN

Pro Dating Tip: If the master bedroom is off-limits, his heart probably is too.

From an outsider's point of view, I suppose it appeared like I was sowing my wild oats. Sure, I was going on many dates and meeting a lot of men, even sleeping with some of them, but I was also experiencing a deep sense of loneliness.

The day I woke up and realized that no one needed me anymore was one of the single most soul-crushing moments in my life. It had only been a couple of months after losing my cats when it occurred to me that no one depended on me for their wellbeing any longer. The feeling of loss and, worse yet, of not being needed was a grief so profound I felt like I was drowning on several occasions.

Online dating was the very distraction I needed at that point. So while distraction was not my initial motivation for accepting the twenty online dates challenge, it involuntarily presented itself as an incentive. I told myself that even if it never worked out, at least I had something to do on a Saturday night, someone to have dinner with.

I met a forty-something half Korean half Japanese man at the popular and overrated Aroma café in Studio City the day after Thanksgiving. My fifth online date was a day date of tea and engaging conversation. Was I immediately physically attracted to him? No. Was I intrigued less than half an hour into the conversation? Yes. Was I concerned that I would stand up with a noticeable puddle of swamp ass on my jeans? Yes, because it was an unseasonably warm holiday weekend.

We chatted about the things that strangers chat about when they're getting to know each other. I.e., likes/dislikes, where one grew up, family, dietary restrictions, etc. When he walked me to my car, I realized how not tall he was, which is a nice way of saying he was short. However, he was handsome in an unconventional way. He definitely worked out, judging by the toned muscles that enveloped me in our goodbye hug and the noticeable veins peeking out from his hairless forearms. This made up for whatever was lacking in the vertical department.

We verbally agreed to "do this again," and he promptly followed through, scoring him points and a second date.

Upon showing my friends his photo, LaChele (the dear friend who reached out to me while in Japan) decided to call him "High Cheeks" due to his strikingly sharp, chiseled jawline.

I made my way to his Venice condo, situated a couple blocks from the beach for our second date. When I asked him if he frequented the beach, his response was a disappointing, "no." If it weren't for his own displeasure, acknowledged in the tone of his response, this would have told me that he's a man who takes things for granted. Once one goes on enough dates, one becomes attuned to seemingly minute details that tell a broader truth.

Upon entering his place, I immediately noticed the lack of windows. I also noticed how neat and nicely decorated it was – white walls, modern décor, and attractive art pieces demanding recognition. There was, without mistake, a financially successful adult man living in this expensive, coastal condo. The heavenly aroma wafting from the kitchen further told me that a man well versed in cooking was living there. Knowing I was a pescetarian, he thoughtfully cooked a delicious meal of salmon and tempura vegetables alongside a salad I happily prepared while he oversaw the vegetables frying on the stove.

Unlike The Doctor, High Cheeks not only owned a rice cooker that he boasted was the best but a whole bunch of other high-tech kitchen gadgets I'd never even heard of. It was impressive, and I was ready to get on Amazon by the end of the night and order a bunch of cool shit for my kitchen that would eventually just collect layers of dust. *But*, if I continued dating High Cheeks, he could get use out of them for me! AKA cook for me often. Listen to me! Only the second date, and I was already making him into my own private chef. What can I say? One of the ways to my heart is through my stomach.

High Cheeks gave me a quick tour of his home. Fascinated by this bachelor's digs, I listened as he described his recently completed renovations. I wanted to suggest he add more light but smartly decided that it probably wasn't a second date's place to be giving unsolicited interior design advice. Sort of the way ordering high-tech kitchen gadgets in the hopes he'll cook for you more often probably isn't appropriate post-second date behavior, either. *But was this dude a vampire*? Two-bedroom, one-bath condo with an open space floor plan, a deep soaking tub, and two measly windows cloaked in overpriced blackout curtains.

He was a fantastic cook who happened to pay the bills with his computer knowledge or something like that. It didn't involve the kitchen, that much I do know. But if he ever wanted to change professions and cook for a living, he certainly could. Shit, if I could afford it, I'd pay him to be my professional cook. But if this didn't last then, that might be awkward.

Hey, I have a date tonight. Can you cook your fancy salmon and tempura vegetables for us? You know the dish you made for me on our second date?

Yup. That's awkward.

After he made me one of the most delectable meals I've ever had, I found myself lying on my back, legs spread, in his guest bedroom. I didn't stay the night. I'd learned that lesson with The Doctor.

High Cheeks wanted to send me home with leftovers, but I reluctantly declined. I was unsure if we would see each other again, and if I took home leftovers, I'd have to return his Tupperware. What if this Tupperware wasn't the basic Ikea shit but some space-age glassware that I couldn't just keep?*

Our third date consisted of an incredible sushi meal in my neck of the woods. He picked a nondescript spot in Sherman Oaks off of Ventura Boulevard. He said he was a friend of the owners, though I never saw any personal interaction happen between him and any restaurant employees. We did feast, though.

"How do you feel about marriage and wedding rings?"

I almost spit out my spicy tuna onto his neatly pressed, white dress shirt. His question freaked me out, though I managed to keep my anxiety to myself, and surprisingly, the sushi in my mouth. It was only the third date, for God's sake! Why the hell were we talking about matrimony? Maybe I *should have* suggested additional lighting for his vampire den.

He followed the question up with how he knew this woman who cheated on the husband after many years. *Ah, insecurity*! It roared and reared its ugly head over rolls of spicy yellowtail and seaweed salad. I wondered if this was the reason a successful, intelligent, reasonably attractive man in his forties had never been married? Maybe he had trust issues? At the same time, I didn't want to over-speculate.

---

*I overthink most things, yes.

A week and a half later, I returned to his coffin, I mean condo, to make pasta from scratch. This would have been a sensual experience if it weren't for the fact that I was beginning to feel weird in his presence. It felt a bit more like work instead of our fourth date, and his sense of humor was either nonexistent or entirely out of sync with my own. I was still attracted to him, or I wouldn't have accepted the peculiar invitation to bathe with him in that deep soaking tub of his after consuming homemade fettuccine.

The bath was *weird*. I feel like bathing with someone is such an intimate experience reserved for those with whom one has become exceptionally close, and I wouldn't describe my relationship with High Cheeks as *close*. Bathing with someone is even more intimate than showering. At least in a shower, you're standing, and it's easier to *fuck*. A bath is such a strange fourth date act, but then again, marriage is such a strange third date conversation, so I can't say I was entirely surprised that High Cheeks would suggest our bathing together.

While sipping an Old-Fashioned, we engaged in underwater foreplay before having boring sex in his guest bedroom. I felt like I was living in an exceptionally mediocre episode of Mad Men. Each time we fucked, it was never in his actual master bedroom. I found this to be very odd when good ol' *Benefit of the Doubt* intervened, "Maybe it's because he shares a wall with his neighbor in his master bedroom." Her frenemy, *Hindsight*, said, "Bitch, please!"

It's important to mention here that I'd already gone on date numero uno with the seventh man I'd met online. And you might be wondering, what about the sixth? I felt like I was "getting good" at this dating thing, whatever that means. I suppose I was able to juggle a couple of guys simultaneously without accidentally calling one of them the wrong name or sending a text to one that was meant for the other.

My dating philosophy had evolved by this time. I decided that there was no harm in seeing more than one man at a time until I found someone worthy of all of my affection and attention. It accelerated my chances of finding that "one" as so many like to deem it, though I prefer to call him my "ride or die."

My ride or die is the person who will have my back no matter what, someone who will be there when my face is swollen and tear-stained with carpet imprints. He's someone who will hold me when I'm crying so hard, I can barely breathe, who will still love me during and after the dark. Scratch that. He'll love me even *more* because that's what my deep heart would do. In other words, I could call him in the middle of the night and tell him I just murdered someone, and he'd ask me how he could help – a loyalty that knew no boundaries. Or, more realistic, my car broke down in the middle of nowhere, and he'd come to get me no matter what time of day or night because, well, I'm not a murderer.

A week after our aquatic action and guest bedroom banging, I heard from High Cheeks via text:

Would you like to go to a Hollywood Hills mansion party this weekend? Bring friends!

No, thank you. I already have plans.

I politely declined, citing plans that I didn't actually have. I just had no interest in going to some bougie Hollywood party with a bunch of forty-something bachelors who text the woman they've been dating and ask her to bring friends to a "Hollywood Hills mansion party." I never saw or heard from High Cheeks again.*

---

*That's not entirely true.

DON'T QUIT YOUR DAY JOB

Pro Dating Tip: The armor may be shiny, but always beware of what lies beneath.

If you're in your late thirties and still trying to make it in Hollywood, you're the reason why I made a rule to swipe whatever way rejects your sorry ass. That aspiration made sense in my twenties. In fact, I dated and fell madly in love with an actor when I was twenty-one. And guess what? He *made it*! Hats off to him.

A former professional baseball player turned aspiring actor at thirty-seven years old suggested we meet at the Coffee Bean down the street from my apartment. The only reason I didn't swipe left on this incredibly good-looking, exceptionally tall, light-skinned Black man was solely physical. By the way, swiping left is the direction that dictates zero connection for all of you who've never experienced an online dating app, which means you were probably in a serious relationship or married before Y2K and/or you've never attempted to live vicariously through your single friend's personal life.

Anyhow, he was *hot*. And at this point in the twenty online dates quest, after blasé sex with High Cheeks and pseudo-makeout sessions with a sweaty wannabe rockstar, I was hot and bothered.

I arrived at the Coffee Bean shortly before online date #6. I'd bought a hot green tea and sat down right before he walked in. He was lean, athletic, and smooth-talking, embracing me with a baritone, "Nice to meet you." He didn't buy anything – no coffee, tea, snack, water – *nothing*.

"Did you wanna get something?" I asked.

"Oh, nah. I don't drink coffee. This is just my go-to first date locale."

Ahem, good to know. (*Insert rolling-eyes-emoji here*).

The conversation revolved around him and his sports days, the stint of work he'd done in a juvenile hall, and how much weed he regularly smoked. He made more than a couple of blatant references to my physique, not only with his words but also with his eyes. Discretion wasn't his strong suit, but I don't think it was a priority either. The only thing gentlemanly about this guy was his ability to hold a door open for me and walk me to my car after our date.

He had three roommates, and he was cheap to boot. If the fact that he didn't purchase anything during our date at Coffee Bean wasn't a telltale sign of this, then the fact that his idea of a second date was "chillin' at his crib" definitely solidified that inference. I'm not one of those women that need my date to pay for everything, either. But his behavior was indicative of so much more.

Post first date, I wasn't too stoked, but I thought, if nothing else, he'd satisfy my bodily needs. I was horny, and I was physically attracted to this guy. I could sleep with him, hoping that he was better in bed than he was at conversation and courting.

When the Friday of our proposed second date rolled around, he texted me that he was stuck in traffic and running slightly late. That was no big deal – we live in LA, after all. I asked him if he'd eaten, letting him know I was at Trader Joe's picking up a few things, including wine. I hadn't eaten, and I was hungry.

I have a frozen pizza in my freezer. You can bring over the wine.

He *assumed* I was purchasing this wine for both of us when, in fact, I was not. I told him I was a pescetarian and didn't eat meat, *assuming* it was probably a pizza fit for a carnivore.

So, what do you want to do?

If a date texted me something like that today, I would probably respond with, "*I don't want to do anything…with you*." Instead, I replied:

Well, I need to eat something so I'm gonna grab dinner real quick.

I was already feeling the uneasiness in the pit of my stomach. That uneasiness, better known as instinct, was kicking in – literally. My smartphone screen lit up:

Ok, no problem. Let me know when you're on your way...Oh, and wear something comfortable.

Excuse me? What kind of man tells a woman to wear something *comfortable*?

I texted him back that I would not be joining him after all, that I was uncomfortable with his attire comment. He proceeded to berate me until the early morning hours with accusations of being "that flake" I professed disdain for during our first date. Instead of apologizing for making me uncomfortable, he was acutely defensive. I knew I'd made the right decision immediately, and I couldn't have been prouder of myself at that moment.

The following morning, he texted me:

Enjoy your day. Oh sorry that might've made you uncomfortable so don't enjoy your day and make sure you wear extremely uncomfortable clothing while doing so. Smh.

I couldn't help but laugh. This was a man in his late thirties behaving like a fucking child - a man child. I hadn't responded to any of Man Child's messages, mind you, since I'd told him why I wasn't coming. I simply took a screenshot of the comedy and prepped for my first date with online date #7.

THE B-WORD AND OTHER BULLSHIT

Pro Dating Tip: If he only wants your egg, ask yourself if he should really pro-create.

Would it be all right if I called?

I was more than eager to take that phone call. I appreciate a human being who understands the value of a conversation dictated by tone and inflection instead of emojis. While dating High Cheeks, I began talking to a thirty-eight-year-old accountant. It was the week of Thanksgiving, and this preppy, 5'10" finance man and I immediately hit it off. I was baking pumpkin pie and answering what I call "getting to know you" questions between cracking eggs and tablespoons of brown sugar. What kind of music do you like? What do you do for a living? What's your favorite food? An hour in, I'd learned he was originally from South Korea, grew up in Los Angeles' South Bay, and currently resided downtown.

We seemed to have much in common, including our love for sushi, and I really liked his voice over the phone. He wanted to take me to one of the best sushi restaurants in LA for our first date the following Saturday. I couldn't wait!

In the week leading up to our date, he asked me for my email. He sent me a Los Angeles Times article on the very restaurant he'd been boasting about since our telephone call. I dug the effort this guy was putting in.

Saturday finally arrived. In the morning, I was actively partaking in my beauty regimen that had become much more high maintenance since I began online dating: Face and hair mask the night before and some yoga before washing away both. A mani/pedi was likely, as well as a touch-up to my eyelash extensions.

As I emerged from my eyelash appointment, I noticed that he'd texted me.

I threw out my back playing golf yesterday. So sorry, but can we reschedule to next weekend?

First of all, *golfing*?! And second, I figured he was blowing me off for a hotter date or something. I politely obliged his request for a rain check, vainly hoping my eyelashes would still be on point a week later.

The same morning I was receiving immature messages from Man Child, I was also having brunch with my best friend. I was filling Norma in on all of my dating shenanigans when my cell phone buzzed.

How are you doing?

It was The Doctor. The last time I'd heard from him, I was boarding a bullet train in Tokyo.

I'm doing really well. Thanks for asking. Long time no speak – how are you doing?

I know...been so busy, but can't complain.

Busy sucking on someone else's toes, I thought to myself.

Let me just take a moment to inform you how much I despise people using "busy" as an excuse or means of small talk. It's not cute, and it means nothing to me because we're all fucking busy. We make time for the things and the people that we want to make time for, so don't inform me that you're busy expecting anything resembling sympathy or understanding in return.

I once read something that resonated and stuck with me since: *Stop glorifying the act of being busy*. The first person that came to mind was my brother. I wanted to insert the descriptive word "estranged" before the noun brother, but when I did that, I just felt like shit. I suppose it doesn't matter, as it's the reality whether or not I want to verbalize it or write it down. My brother was the king of "busy." He'd milked that term to death and eventually alienated himself and his family into a far corner of northern Michigan, where he chose not to give anyone in his deceased parents' family his address.

Every time anyone, or in this case, the first guy I ever went on an online date with, reaches out to me after a while and begins with, "I'm sorry. I've just been so busy," I actively cringe. I don't need to hear that. The fact that you reached out, regardless of how much time has passed, is enough. Let's just start with, "Hi, I've been thinking about you. How are you doing?"

While we're on the topic of reaching out to someone, I also detest small talk. I want to dive deeper, talk about things that matter. I don't care how hot the weather has been unless we're discussing global warming, but I do care how you have dreams about living somewhere with all four seasons. I want to know there's a purpose behind why you're asking me how my day was. *Especially* if I've fucked you before!

If The Doctor wanted to ask me how I was doing, tell me he's busy, and then ask me out again, perhaps I could ease up on my qualms about the b-word. But he didn't. I didn't bother replying to his message, and less than a month later, he stopped following me on Instagram. Good riddance!

Back to online date #7: It was an early December evening, warm the way Southern California days are during that time of year, the lukewarm one feels when turning both the hot and cold water on at the same time. It was a week after his golfing injury when we finally met. He was standing outside waiting for me when I arrived at his place. I was parking near his home to Uber together to the restaurant in Little Tokyo.

He was wearing dark blue jeans and a light grey cashmere sweater with the sleeves rolled up, exposing his hairless, muscular forearms. His espresso brown, almost black hair was parted on the side, neatly combed. I was oddly and instantly attracted to his preppy appearance. His assertiveness and the fact that he'd made all the plans were admirable and a turn-on. I was impressed by his visible charisma and chivalry. As we awaited the arrival of our Uber driver and I caught first sight of his thin-lipped smirk that revealed charming dimples, I thought to myself, *I'm going to sleep with this man.*

We shared a boozy pitcher of sangria while waiting for a coveted seat at the sushi bar of the Japanese restaurant I'd been anticipating for two weeks. Conversing about our travels, the single dating life, and yummy food, the laughs were abundant and the flirting effortless. I was relaxed, sincerely enjoying his company.

Dinner was spectacular, reminiscent of meals I'd partaken in during my recent trip to Japan. This man's fabulous taste in quality sushi and friendliness with the chef certainly scored him points. Between decadent bites of salmon collar and spicy tuna, I relayed how much I appreciated his effort to actually call me on the phone as opposed to just texting. When the bill came, I offered to pay for half while pulling out my wallet.

"Thank you, but please put away your wallet." He motioned with his hand politely.

After dinner, he grabbed dessert while I enjoyed a matcha latte. His ice cream was the only thing he'd allow me to pay for, and even this was noticeably difficult for him. Dinner wasn't cheap, and as I mentioned earlier, I'm not the type of woman who expects a man to pay for everything. Is it nice to be treated? Yes. Do I appreciate it? Absolutely. Am I still going to pull out my wallet and offer? *Every time*.

He asked if I'd like to come back to his place to sober up before driving home. I eagerly obliged.

His place was really nice, well suited for the bachelor's life. While it lacked art, it was clean, which is essential. I can't tell you how many times I've scolded women *and* men for this very thing. Someone will say to me she's dating so and so and "their place is a pigsty, but..." and that's where I cut her off because I know she's about to tell me she's still planning on seeing this person and/or justify the fact that they live in squalor.

Let me tell you something: If you're a grown-ass man or woman and you can't do dishes, or you leave half-eaten food on the coffee table for days to the point that your place smells, if your toilet looks like you don't have a clue what a toilet brush looks like, let alone own one, there is a much deeper issue at hand. There are no buts, people. *Just. Run. Out. The. Door*! I understand every now and then we all get a little behind on household chores, but there's a big difference between not having time to do the laundry and dirty boxer briefs that have been in between the cushions of someone's couch for weeks. Trust me.

Another glass of wine later, we were making out on his sofa.

"We're not having sex, but we can fool around, right?" He asked in between tongue-tying kisses.

I, and my nether regions, agreed that fooling around was a welcomed activity. We may as well have had sex on our first date, though we did not - just about everything else *but*.

We went bike riding at Redondo Beach's pier on our second date. It was a beautiful, cool December evening, and while the sunset and beach fare were lovely, the anticipation of what the night had in store was obviously on both of our minds.

"I'm looking forward to taking you back to my place." He said with a cheesy smile.

"That sentiment is mutual," I ran my fingers through his thick, dark hair as we drove northbound on the 110 with the windows down, enjoying the breeze.

We showered individually, washing away the sea salt and sweat from the day's activities. He'd lit candles and turned on Majid Jordan's *The Space Between* album for background music as I emerged from the bathroom. My clothes didn't stay on long.

TURKEY BASTERS AND DUIs

We'd gone on less than a handful of dates when I found out how important it was for this man to become a father. As he passionately exclaimed how a family was something he always wanted, my heart sank. It *plummeted* into my stomach. I mean, sure, he'd told my best friend that he was my boyfriend early on without us ever having discussed exclusivity, but I now had to tell him about my decision to have a tubal ligation! I already felt strong feelings for him. I could sense the feelings were mutual, and here I was, *spayed,* like a housecat. My mind raced, and perhaps my decision to relay this to him was as impulsive as my decision to have the surgery. Still, I wasn't about to string him along. Mr. Baby Crazy deserved an out *now* rather than later after things potentially got more serious. He didn't take the out.

As the holidays approached, Mr. Baby Crazy and I celebrated our birthdays together while Mr. East Coast and I exchanged birthday cards and well wishes. We were all December babies. Mr. East Coast sent me a gift that got lost in snail mail transit, something he'd picked up during his solo travels to Morocco. He was really upset with the postal service's fuck up, so while in Seattle during the holiday with his family, he picked up another trinket for me in the Pike Place market. He mailed it to me with a sweet note stating that he thought of me, and my style of décor, when he saw it. He felt it fitting to send to me in place of his lost Moroccan gem. While kind, I thought it an odd gesture coming from the man not looking for a commitment. This peripheral affection was not conducive to what I was looking for, but at the time, I was making a conscious effort not to overthink things.

Mr. Baby Crazy and I celebrated New Year's Eve together while Mr. East Coast and I bid one another Happy New Year through text message. By the new year, I'd met most of Mr. Baby Crazy's closest friends, and he'd spent only a couple of hours with mine, a fact that left me slightly perturbed.

Our relationship consisted of a healthy dose of excellent sushi and frequent sex. On a dinner date in early January, over bites of takoyaki, Mr. Baby Crazy casually relayed to me that he'd had his office receptionists pick out my birthday gift. That was one of the first dumb things he ever told me. There was no reason for me to know that absolutely no thought from him went into picking out my gift. He got a pass because I didn't expect anything from him in the first place. He'd gifted me a leather Rebekah Minkoff clutch from Bloomingdale's the night of my birthday party. I silently took issue with the fact that the clutch was genuine leather, and I'm a pescatarian, mindful of not purchasing products made from animal parts. But being that it was a gift, I maintained tact and appreciation for the act of being given anything. For the record, I shipped him wine from his favorite Napa winery because I paid attention when he told me how much he loved this particular estate.

"Really? You wouldn't want a little one of you like that running around?" he asked one afternoon while walking around downtown's Japanese Village Plaza. He was referring to the adorable sibling girls of mixed Asian and European races that had just run past us on their way to the pastry shop. These references continued for weeks, every chance he got. There was an element of sweetness to some of the comments, but I began feeling pressured. I really wanted this guy to get it through his seemingly thick skull that, *no, I didn't want a little one of me running around anywhere – not now, not ever*!

I'd willingly given up my ability to become pregnant in the "natural" way, but I could still be fertilized. As a teenager, when I knew then that I didn't want children, my aunt would joke that if I ever changed my mind and didn't have a sperm donor, AKA a man, there was always the "turkey baster." For this pescatarian, the thought of my child being born of an instrument that coats meat with its own juices is repulsive.

Mr. Baby Crazy was a planner, and while that certainly had its downside, it also relieved me of those duties from time to time. I appreciated that a lot of our time spent together didn't take much effort on my part. He genuinely seemed to like taking care of me, and while being taken care of was unique in my world, I was learning how to appreciate it.

By the end of February, almost three months into dating, we dressed to the nines and celebrated "Un-Valentine's Day," as he called it. His version of the commercial holiday started with a dozen roses sent to my work on February twentieth, followed by an indulgent, delicious seafood dinner at the fancy downtown Water Grill and a long elevator ride to the top of the Intercontinental Hotel. The amazing view from their rooftop bar alone would have been worth the trip, but we took a seat at the bar for one more drink.

It was there, over glasses of rosé, he told me he'd been considering a life without children ever since I told him that I didn't want any. I returned the sentiment. I, too, had been reconsidering my childless future. I felt like this was our way of telling each other we were in it for the long haul, and I appreciated his willingness to broach the topic. We were going to figure this out because what we shared wasn't worth losing over a point in the future that we were nowhere even near. He was nearing forty, however, and I knew he was a lot more eager to figure it out than I was, not only emotionally but biologically.

A couple of weeks after our Un-Valentine's Day, I wanted to repay the efforts he'd gone to, so I planned a surprise weekend getaway to Santa Barbara. On the ride up, during the one-lane San Marcos pass into Santa Ynez wine country, I gave him a blowjob while he drove the relatively secluded, winding highway. I wore my seatbelt the whole time, which uncomfortably dug into my hip under my awkward lean over the center console. I silently couldn't wait for him to cum, so I could regain some personal comfort. When we arrived at our first destination, his white t-shirt had smudges of my makeup on it, which conjured up an impish mutual giggle.

At the winery, we shared a couple bottles of wine and a picnic I'd packed for the occasion. We people watched, snapping cute photos of our spread to send to our frequent social companions, his best friend, and his best friend's wife.

The conversation segued to children again. Thus arrived the killjoy.

"Think about it! You could still hang out with your girlfriends because my mom would be an amazing caregiver, and I'd willingly stay home with the baby on occasion!"

Oh, gee, I thought, *a father who'd actually take care of his child – what a novel idea*!

"You can take as much time off as you'd like after having the baby, too!" He enthusiastically continued his fantasy as if this was the magical incentive that would untie my tubes.

"How much time are you talking?" I was curious.

"Five years."

The bewildered look upon my face must have said more than any words I could have uttered because he quickly followed that up with, "five months?"

"That's more like it," I stated, rolling my eyes and drinking my wine that I wouldn't be able to drink and that I would miss very much, *especially* if I were pregnant with this man's child.

I tried to keep an open mind, thinking of my dear mother, who often told me how much she wished she could have been a stay-at-home mother. She wanted to be present for almost everything, but financial burden never would've allowed for it. Given the circumstances, I'd say she did a pretty damn good job.

I tried appreciating Mr. Baby Crazy's commitment to painting a picture of a happy, healthy, and financially stable future family. But I just couldn't shake the anxiety at the thought that his future was sooner than later, and mine was much more Sci-Fi futuristic. Like, cars flying already futuristic. I couldn't rid myself of the thought of being the stay-at-home mom who one day regretted losing her career while her husband is off sleeping with his secretary, the very secretary who helps pick out her annual, unethical birthday gift.

We went to one more winery before checking into our oceanfront hotel.

"The next woman I introduce to my parents is going to be the woman I marry," Mr. Baby Crazy promised himself after his last relationship ended.

He relayed this to me in our inebriated stupor, shaded by a beautiful, old oak tree on the winery's outdoor deck. We were sipping

Chardonnay overlooking a picturesque panorama of pastoral rolling hills and grapevines.

Later that night, we had dinner at the delicious Toma, an Italian restaurant where we ate like royalty - Grilled octopus, some fancy tuna appetizer, margherita flatbread, gnocchi, and another *unnecessary* bottle of wine. It was there that the day's worth of vino consumption caught up to my emotions, and some of my dark seeped out. Mr. Baby Crazy was unsure of how to handle this. However, he did a pretty good job.

"I can't imagine becoming a mother in a world where my mother no longer exists," I told him in between suppressing tears.

As much as I learned how to stand on my own two feet after her death, I didn't trust many of my decisions about men, let alone a helpless little life. What if I had a child with a man, and the relationship didn't work out in the end? Could I withstand another loss without the presence of my mother's unwavering strength and support? I probably underestimated my strength, but I didn't want to find out.

We took an Uber back to the hotel, where we showered and went to sleep. He wasn't a fan of "drunk sex," and I'm pretty sure I was in no condition for sexual activity. Morning sex was on the table*, however.

We ended our Santa Barbara weekend getaway by meeting his young cousin for ramen. He was attending college at the local university, and Mr. Baby Crazy wanted to say hi, introduce me, and hand him five hundred dollars.

I was having several thoughts during all of this and not necessarily in this order:

- I wish someone would've handed me five hundred dollars when I was going to college.
- I'm not really a fan of ramen; udon is way better.
- I didn't just get introduced to his parents, but he did introduce me to a family member. Is Mr. Baby Crazy trying to tell me something? Nah, he probably just really wanted to give his cousin money.

It was as if my presence wasn't noticeable. I sat and picked at my ramen while he and his cousin engaged in small talk and adolescent male banter. Mr. Baby Crazy didn't even try to include me in the conversation.

---

* We didn't literally have sex on the table, although that would have been fun.

I didn't finish my ramen, and I was hungry an hour later. Did I mention that was our first meal of the day? Yes, we had ramen for breakfast – not exactly my idea of the breakfast of champions.

Snowboarding, golfing, and Mr. Baby Crazy's second job helping his brother with his marijuana business began taking priority over quality time spent with me. I, naturally, vocalized my concerns.

We had our first real spat after he listed all of the reasons he preferred not coming to or staying over at my place. One of those reasons was the most telling: he didn't like the art in my bedroom, which was skeletons printed on dictionary pages expressing love.

"It's just so dark," he commented.

I agreed to take them down if he agreed to come to my place more often. It was called compromise. I'd be lying, though, if I didn't tell you how much of a bitch I thought he was for being bothered by some "dark" art. It was fucking art and some of my favorite, I might add.

Another reason he cited was that my place was "cold." *Boohoo*, put on a goddamned jacket - this selfish guy has got to be kidding me! (*Insert eye-rolling emoji here*). I began asking myself if I really wanted this man to be the father of any children I might consider having in my future?

One night, my phone rang as it usually did somewhere between 9:30 and 10:30. Mr. Baby Crazy was driving home from Santa

Monica. The slurring was audible. He was drunk. I asked him where he was, and thankfully, he was almost home.

I was so angry for so many reasons. Not only for driving drunk but also because I was now an accomplice. I was angry that, years prior, he'd received a DUI. Clearly, he hadn't learned his lesson! I was angry that one of my friends lost her mother to a drunk driver and that in 2005, I had to pick up two dear friends in the middle of the night in Hollywood when a drunk driver struck them. Not to mention, I spent many nights of my childhood wondering if my alcoholic father was lying dead in a ditch somewhere, followed by many nights during my marriage, worried that my alcoholic husband was too.

I asked Mr. Baby Crazy to call me when he got home. He didn't call me until the following morning. I realized that night that the only skeletons he was really afraid of were the ones in his own closet.

"You could have killed yourself or someone else! I was married to an alcoholic. My father was a substance abuser. *You've had a DUI before*! Do you take anything seriously?"

I continued to rattle off the barrage of worries and concerns I had that surrounded his behavior, with the intent of conveying how much I cared about him. He claimed he understood, though I think I was being placated. Had I used our theoretical children in my plight, perhaps that would have been more successful, but I certainly didn't want to get his baby crazy hopes up.

Weeks began to pass full of our pleasant routine: A good morning call or text message followed by a potential midday lunch text and a phone call between nine and ten at night. Although most of these exchanges were so brief and unfulfilling, I was grateful for their consistency, until I didn't receive my goodnight phone call one night. Mr. Baby Crazy had run into an old female friend, who invited him to happy hour. Happy hour extended well past the hours of 5-7pm, and he later justified his actions with the following:

"I took an Uber – aren't you proud? And I'm not even attracted to her! Besides, you know I don't like having sex while intoxicated." (*Insert eye-rolling emoji here*). Again, with the dumb-ass comments.

Our weekends were usually spent together or at least one of the days (Fri-Sun) that weren't designated for his golf or snowboarding. Sometimes I would even stay over during weekdays or "school nights." I didn't mind going to his place and spending my time there, but it was the principle of the fact that he still wasn't making an effort to stay at my place.*

---

*I couldn't help but think that if my fur babies were still alive, the scenario would have been very different. It simply wouldn't have been possible because I never would've neglected my animals.

One particular Sunday, Mr. Baby Crazy decided he needed a new pair of shoes, so we went to the mall. We perused aisles of Nike and Adidas, golf paraphernalia, and sports uniforms. I learned about his history of playing baseball, a sport much more exciting than one involving a titanium club.

"I still have my uniform somewhere."

"Oooh, you'll have to try that on for me some time," I responded, feeling way more excited than I was during the previous conversation we had about the different qualities of golf ball brands.

"Only if you put on your cheerleading uniform for me."

I didn't have my cheerleading uniform anymore, so I knew our little fantasy would never exceed the brick and mortar of Dick's Sporting Goods. After buying me a black Los Angeles Dodgers baseball cap, we perused the shoe stores. The mall was really packed that afternoon, and I felt the familiar anxiety I usually experience in enclosed, busy spaces. As he went to pay for his shoes, I needed more open space, so I told him I'd be right outside.

As I neared the railing of the second floor, I noticed a giant banner hanging from the ceiling advertising the hospital that The Doctor worked at. On the poster were doctors posing for a photo, which one would expect to just be stock photos, but *could it be*? I squinted and searched the faces of the group shot. Yes, it was him – my very first online date ever. Arms folded in front of his white coat, stethoscope draped around his burly neck, and a slight but serious smile across his face. I quickly snapped a photo and sent it to my girlfriends asking:

Do you see what I see?

"Ready to go?"

I jumped only slightly when Mr. Baby Crazy came up behind me. He hadn't seen me take the photo, thank God. I don't know how I would have explained that one.

Um, I'm thinking about getting arthroplasty, or the truth: *that handsome Asian doctor in that photo once had my toes in his mouth. I was sending a picture to my girlfriends because this kinda shit only happens to me.*

One night, after a date of heavy drinking and socializing in a swanky hotel bar in downtown LA with his best friend's wife, Mr. Baby Crazy and I arrived back at his place late.

"I can't believe I'm telling you this, but" He began.

I was nervous about what was coming next because of his deplorable knack for saying really dumb shit. But unfortunately, my response time was impaired by several glasses of overpriced red wine.

"With you, there are no buts," he finished.

I breathed a slight sigh of relief, though inquisitive.

I learned there were always buts in his previous relationships, especially before three months. From the little he'd shared, he was nitpicking his way through women, once claiming that Mickey Mouse had something to do with his previous failed relationships.

"The last two relationships I've been in both ended shortly after I took them to Disneyland." He informed me after I told him I wasn't a fan of the theme parks.

I started wondering if maybe, like Mr. East Coast, he was afraid of commitment. Mr. Baby Crazy repeatedly reminded me how he hadn't had a relationship make it past three months in years. Great, I would think while simultaneously wondering what this meant for us. And trust me when I tell you he had our three-month anniversary marked on a calendar somewhere, even if only in his head. Then one evening, a coworker of his who I'd just met asked if I was aware of Mr. Baby Crazy's "three-month hang up." His obsession was apparently public knowledge.

"How could I forget about your three-month achievement? You won't let me!" I scoffed.

It began feeling like Mr. Baby Crazy was more concerned with reaching numeric milestones in relation to his past than the more meaningful milestones in our relationship. I think there were lots of buts for me:

But he wants kids, and I don't.

But he values money more than he values relationships.

But he's a workaholic.

But he says really stupid things before thinking sometimes.

But I don't feel like a priority in his life.

The same night of his "no buts" declaration, he also referred to relationships as "business transactions."* Of course, everything was a business transaction to this man. Relationships were a fucking Excel spreadsheet to him! He really knew how to *Delete* the romance from everything where *Save As* would have fucking sufficed.

I was in the bathroom brushing my teeth and getting ready for bed when he walked in, farted, and walked out chortling. It was the first time he'd ever deliberately farted in front of me. I ran out of the bathroom, scolding him with my revulsion.

I didn't want him to be comfortable passing gas in my presence, let alone do it on purpose. I wanted him to be comfortable letting me in on some of that darkness he was harboring. I wanted him to tell me about his fears and insecurities, preferably while sober.

"If we're going to get married, I should be able to comfortably fart in front of you," he stated.

I was instantly more affected by the word married than his deliberate farting. Even with all the baby talk, marriage rarely entered the conversation aside from when he mentioned that the next woman

---

*Add that to the List of Dumb Things Mr. Baby Crazy says.

he introduced to his parents would be the woman he married. That statement was more indirect, whereas this was very much about us.

I sighed, turned, and walked out of the room at a loss for words. Our previous argument was now clouded with legal documents and unnecessarily expensive celebrations that would only serve to put one in debt and probably end in divorce. Nevertheless, it was clear I had some unaddressed issues.

The disappointment in his conducting relationships as business transactions and literally planning out every single thing weighed heavy. The spontaneity and adventure seemingly present at the beginning of our relationship had vanished. He was predictable, the excitement nonexistent - Even where our sex life was concerned. He would often watch ESPN, smoke a joint followed by a cigarette, brush his teeth and exclaim, “Sexy Time” with a clap of his hands. Thankfully, I was usually already in bed, expecting sex to commence. Besides the fact that I was rarely invited to smoke a joint with him, there was nothing less sexy about his behavior. It felt scheduled, thus losing a great deal of its appeal. At least he never had bad breath from smoking those cancer sticks – at least there was that.

WHITE NOISE

I really began feeling like Mr. Baby Crazy was hiding something, that there was more to him than his put-together, successful, well-dressed, handsome exterior suggested. And this feeling began affecting the lightness that much of our relationship existed upon.

After three months of dating, it seemed kind of ridiculous that we hadn't exchanged social media information. Whenever I brought it up, he'd get defensive. His excuse was that he barely ever posts anything and that he really only uses his Instagram for snowboarding videos blah blah blah. Bullshit Radar *activated*.

My familiarity with death, my non-existent relationship with my brother, and my divorce were Mr. Baby Crazy's idea of dark, which started to become a blockade. He'd often label me as "complex." I knew that his projections meant that he, too, had some dark, if not more, and I was the easiest target.

"Haven't you had any friends who've experienced some sort of trauma?" I asked him.

"No, not really. A buddy of mine's dad got cancer and died. That's about it."

This seemed strange to me and made me realize that he was probably avoiding the dark with everyone, not just me. Someone who consistently shied away from any depth or darkness is definitely avoiding some demon, and *I wanted in*. I wanted to shake hands with that demon and get to know him. I've been around long enough to know that the success of a relationship is, oftentimes, dependent upon how much a person is willing to allow themselves to be vulnerable.

During one of our first real fights, I aggressively asked him, "What do you want?"

"I want a family."

"So, basically, you just want my egg?" I retorted.

I knew family, for him, meant kids. He'd made it very clear that he'd been longing to spread his seed with the first willing female, preferably of European descent. Not only was it a biological accomplishment in his mind, but it would also make his very religious Korean parents proud. In other words, his priorities were askew.

"What do you want?" he asked, seemingly confused as to why I would be appalled by his sole reasoning for being in our relationship.

"I want my ride or die, someone to spend time with and experience my life with who isn't just looking for me to have his babies and spend his money."

The fact that I would end up dating an almost forty-year-old, wealthy man who *really* wanted children was comical. And not in the ha-ha sort of way but more like a tragic comedy. I knew there was some sort of takeaway from this experience. I just didn't quite grasp what it was yet.

One night while discussing his anxiety and obsession with almost reaching the three-month milestone, he informed me that he'd already picked out a date for when I'd meet his parents.

"Six months from today, September 1st."

"September 1st, huh?"

Had he penciled it in the day I told him my tubes were tied, I wondered?

I was fucking irritated. This clearly meant he wanted a future with me, but I became a checked box on his list of things to do because he couldn't just say those things directly, like a normal human being. All of the romance, or what was left of it, was wholly expunged. It was prime passive-aggressive behavior. I truly was a fucking business transaction to this idiot.

"And I was hoping you might not wear so many rings when you meet them." Mr. Baby Crazy admitted.

Shock replaced anxiety, and I wished he hadn't waited three months to attempt to change me. So, naturally, I questioned his unexpected request, at which point he cited "cultural differences" as a means of justification. How was I to argue with that? Well, I did.

"What else do you want to change about me?"

"I was also hoping you could remove your nose ring. You can put it back in after you meet them."

The words rolled off his tongue so nonchalantly while I sat on the other side of the phone, appalled, my anger boiling. *Who the fuck did he think he was*?

The softening of these blows was supposed to lie in that I was being granted permission to accessorize upon the second meet and greet. In other words, I could be myself. These accessories held sentimental value. I began questioning the logic in that if I remove all of these things that are a part of my daily life, albeit material, how would it look upon our second meeting, at which point I'm decked out in silver, gold, and turquoise? He argued that he didn't want any distraction from what I meant to him. I argued that he could communicate how much I meant to him before our meeting. My jewelry wouldn't even be a contributing factor, much less a distraction.

"It's just white noise that I don't need to hear," he disputed, inferring that his parents would fill his ear with the sins and impurities that are my accessories.

"If you truly accept me for who I am, then you should be able to put up with a little white noise," I stood my ground, becoming audibly agitated.

This man didn't accept me for me. How could I make this mistake? Hadn't I learned *anything*?

I continued the debate telling him that I was uncomfortable presenting a false image to his parents, especially upon the first impression. My communication was met with sharp pangs of simultaneous disappointment and sadness. The argument became ridiculous, and I ended it when I considered that we were quarreling over an event that wasn't occurring until well into the future. And at that point, it didn't seem likely we'd even make it to said event.

IT AIN'T OVER 'TIL IT'S OVER

The night after the jewelry debate, I went out drinking with some acquaintances and friends. I decided to invite Mr. Baby Crazy to join because I believed that being part of an adult relationship didn't mean ignoring someone for days after a disagreement. He thankfully took an Uber. He hit it off with everyone with his charming banter, though I wondered if paying for everyone's liquor had something to do with it?

His love for snowboarding caught the attention of a close male friend of mine named James. James was one of the few solid male figures in my life, and it had been that way for almost six years. He and I, both divorced artists, had swapped many stories and much-solicited relationship advice over countless happy hours and lunches. Standing six feet tall and fit, he was also very easy on the eyes. With his tough-looking tiger tattoos covering almost a quarter of his light brown skin and his black hair framing his large, almond-colored mischievous eyes, he was no doubt the object of many women's fantasies.

Many of my own fantasies starred James, but I always quickly reminded myself what good friends we'd become. No sane woman ever sabotages a friendship with what could end up a mere three minutes of mediocre dick.

James and Mr. Baby Crazy began planning snowboarding dates to Mammoth Lakes. I was oddly jealous because I was never invited on these wintry trips. But the fact that my friends were approving of Mr. Baby Crazy was more important to me than spending time in the freezing ass cold with him.

Later on in the evening, I found myself sitting next to James. We were engaged in conversation while Mr. Baby Crazy explained the ins and outs of Microsoft Excel to a friend of mine. I had to use the restroom, and when I returned, Mr. Baby Crazy had taken my seat next to James, so I sat down next to a colleague. I found this odd. The thought that Mr. Baby Crazy might be jealous flickered through my mind, and I thought, *eh, a little jealousy is good for him.* He needed to think more about the quality of our relationship than his end goal of spreading his seed.

I tried to create peace between us by compromising: I wouldn't remove all of my jewelry but some. The turquoise ring my mother bought from an indigenous tribe near the Grand Canyon and gifted me for my college graduation was staying on. While I may not understand his cultural divide, he couldn't understand losing the most important person in his life. Those material things become precious relics.

As the night wore on well past happy hour, Mr. Baby Crazy took his leave first. I was hoping I'd be invited to go home and spend the night with him, but that didn't happen. I was disappointed, a feeling I was becoming more and more familiar with while dating him.

People's safe opinions of him didn't flood in until the following week. The general consensus was that he was a nice guy. I didn't care about nice! Of course, he was *nice*, especially during first impressions! I cared about the other insights, the ones people aren't always inclined to share for fear of offending.

"I think he enjoys using his wealth as a means, perhaps his only means, to connect with others," James told me that he could tell Mr. Baby Crazy talked a big game.

Finally, some refreshing honesty! I no longer felt like I might be imagining things.

In early March, Mr. Baby Crazy was supposed to have dinner with his brother and then come stay the night at my place. It was a Friday night, and he showed up at my place completely wasted, which meant he'd driven drunk again. Our plan was to go to a nearby wine bar, and we did, though not without my reconsidering our outing given his blatant inebriation. He'd already had too much to drink, but the many times I've tried reasoning with a drunk over the years and failed are abundant. Reason is non-existent with drunks, and I had no interest in exerting that type of energy. After our first serious conversation regarding this type of behavior, it was clear this would be an ongoing struggle. Whether or not I wanted to partake in the said struggle had yet to be determined, considering my history with men who have alcohol-related issues.

We took a short Uber ride to a Burbank wine bar, where he stole a wine cork out of a plastic bucket on the bar. I watched him grab it, throw it in the pocket of his suit jacket, and then giggle sort of the way he giggled when he farted and ran out of the room. I actually thought his thievery was funny, seeing as how the guy who made six figures decided pocketing a $10 plastic wine cork was a better idea than being a paying customer.

He then began boisterously speaking to the owner and other patrons around us.

"Am I embarrassing you?" he asked me.

I wasn't embarrassed, though I'd never seen him like that. He was usually much more reserved in public places unless his friends were present. It was becoming clear that I wasn't the only one cognizant of his blatant inebriation. I managed to get him to focus on the unique, wine-inspired décor.

"We'll have something like this in our future home." He said, referring to the towering floor to ceiling in-wall wine rack behind us.

I smiled, pleased with his brief vision of a future that didn't include a tiny human.

"I don't really consider myself attractive, Lindsay. I see you with someone more like James…tall, dark…handsome with tattoos…" he trailed off, sipping his red wine and staring at the sconces made out of wine bottles on the wood-planked wall behind the bar.

I knew it! He was jealous of him. I was taken aback by the sudden change in subject, assuring him that if I wanted to be with James, I wouldn't be standing in the middle of a wine bar on a Friday night with him. I also told him that I thought he was one of the most handsome men I'd ever laid eyes on. It was all the truth.

A drunken Mr. Baby Crazy decided that while his inhibitions were down, he might as well express another insecurity. He blubbered something about a sex video of my ex-husband and me that he swore was on my laptop at home. He'd claimed he'd seen the thumbnail the last time we watched a movie in bed together. What Mr. Baby Crazy thought he saw was actually a photo of an almost ten-year-old close-up of my best friend, Sandy, and me. Our arms were wrapped around each other at my twenty-second birthday party. No matter how I tried explaining this to him, his mind was made up.

A couple weekends after the date night debacle, I spent the entire day with him while feeling completely and utterly lonely. He sat on his couch, higher than a kite, watching every sport he could find on television, aimlessly channel surfing during commercials. I was bored and desired to be outside enjoying the perfectly gorgeous, sunshine-soaked Sunday. He didn't even notice or offer. Hell, he didn't even ask if I'd like to get high with him.

A week later, it was Sandy's 40th birthday, the same friend from the desktop thumbnail. I surprised her with a weekend getaway to Fallbrook, California. Then I broke up with Mr. Baby Crazy while conversing on the phone in a state of my own complete intoxication.

REBOUNDING WITH A CAPITAL "R"

Less than twenty-four hours after my weepy, drunken breakup, I was on the phone with Mr. East Coast, sending him scantily-clad photos of myself posing emo by the hot tub in my bikini. I made certain he knew my plans to be in New York City that forthcoming Memorial Day. I hoped to see him, sleep with him and spend time with him. He was equally as excited, and this was just the attention and the distraction I needed from the drama that had ensued in the sloppy early morning of what was supposed to be a weekend of celebration.

On the way home from Fallbrook, Sandy and I decided to prolong the weekend. After getting drunk at a random bar, she took an Uber ride home. I met "Brian the Hawaiian," which is what he went into my phone contacts as. We connected over short-lived past love stories and an intellectual conversation about why humans choose the types of partners they choose.

It was getting late when he offered to drive me home in my car then Uber back to his home in Monrovia. Mind you, these were not short distances. Aside from the fact that these two locations are nowhere near one another, sober Lindsay would never have allowed this. Thankfully, this wasn't a bad man, and if my mother were still around, I would get a swift kick in the ass for my decision to accept his offer.

He kissed me outside the bar as we took our leave and then kissed me again after leaving my place, where he awaited his expensive Uber. Well aware that he was a rebound, he still wanted to take me on a date the following weekend. It was nice to have the attention of other men in the aftermath of the debacle that was Mr. Baby Crazy. I accepted Brian the Hawaiian's invitation.

Saturday morning rolled around, and I canceled on him. I lied and told him I was "under the weather." The truth was I wasn't ready. I was still aching over the breakup that occurred while under the influence. Mr. Baby Crazy felt like the first adult relationship I'd been in where futures were discussed, and plans were made since my ex-husband eight years prior. However, I wasn't acting like an adult when I ended things with him.

Less than twenty-four hours after Brian the Hawaiian kissed me, Mr. Baby Crazy showed up at my door with a Trader Joe's grocery bag full of my belongings.

"Um, we need to talk," he said with this bewildered, puppy dog look upon his face that I just wanted to grab and kiss. I felt vulnerability creep in like a sleuth. I invited him in. We sat down at my dining table, where we weighed our options for an hour.

"What if we stay in touch until my work life isn't so crazy? I still want to know how you're doing, but in the meantime, you can do whatever you want."

What in the actual fuck was he suggesting? Was he implying that I could date, make out with, and potentially sleep with all the Brian the Hawaiians* I wished to until his schedule was conducive to being in a relationship? I'm certain this came with terms* that cited he shouldn't be made aware of any of my shenanigans, and he, too, could do the same.

This was absurd to me, and I let him know first, with my befuddled expression, and second, with my words.

I recalled a past conversation where I asked him if he was disappointed that I wasn't Korean. He told me that it was the exact opposite, that he was glad I wasn't Korean. Looking back, I think that had more to do with my genetic makeup than it did with me as an individual with my customs and values. His desire to have a mixed baby, a "Eurasian," as he called it, was disturbingly apparent. After discovering his IG handle and the hundreds of ass-centric accounts he publicly followed, this became even more disturbing. Many of the

---

*Of course, I didn't actually tell Mr. Baby Crazy about Brian the Hawaiian.

*He'd probably keep an Excel spreadsheet on the parts he was privy to.

big-bootied women were mixed race and some unnervingly young looking.

"You were looking for something much different than me," I started, "And then you found me, and you liked me, but you don't know what to do with me. I'm not what you're used to. I'm not Korean, and I'm not going to stay at home with your babies, spend your money, and go to church with your parents on Sunday. I'm also not going to take off my jewelry and be someone I'm not. So let me do us both a favor and end this right now."

Sometimes it's difficult to know if what we want and what we need is synonymous. I've spent many a dollar and many an hour fighting against this very phenomenon. But, in any case, I think Mr. Baby Crazy needed a good Korean Christian woman to take home to mom and dad on September 1st, preferably one whose only jewelry is the princess-cut diamond he puts on her finger.

YOU'RE VERY PRETTY

Pro Dating Tip: Chances are we've all been someone's rebound before, so enjoy yours while you can.

Two weeks after Mr. Baby Crazy and I called it quits, I was ready to adopt the first feline that meowed in my path. I teetered dangerously somewhere between a four-legged furry friend and a one-way flight to a Mediterranean country where the fine men were just as abundant as the fine wine. Thankfully, I was able to see the bright light at the end of a dark tunnel that rendered me regretfully impulsive in the past. No animals were adopted, no flights were booked, no phone calls were made, and no 2am drunk text messages were sent.

All of the above was applause-worthy or at least pat-on-the-back worthy. It's perfectly human to want to shelter homeless animals and send drunken text messages to undeserving exes. And anyone who denies ever being in a similarly vulnerable situation is either allergic to animals and/or perpetually sober.

I did the next best thing - I started swiping, mostly left, on Coffee Meets Bagel until I saw The Englishman. Online date #8 took place at my neighborhood bar, the Red Door. Maybe he'd come galloping in upon his stallion, scoop me up in his knighted arms, and...yeah, I'll stop there.

The Red Door was within walking distance to my home, so I could have walked if I wanted to, and I could booze it up as much as I liked, if necessary.

My phone lit up with a text message from The Englishman while I was parking my car:

I'm the black man sitting at the bar.

I smiled. This was a lovely, much-needed distraction from the small part of me that was still considering adopting a helpless feline. It should be noted that my sadness had less to do with Mr. Baby Crazy himself and more to do with my own self-judgments about not breaking the cycle of choosing emotionally unavailable men. I eased some of that self-loathing with the fact that it only took five months as opposed to five years for me to figure this one out. Maybe I was learning something after all!

The Englishman and I were sitting in a dark corner of the small bar. We shared the crimson velvet cushion underneath us, our legs crossed toward one another, the occasional hand grazing arm or shoulder, and torsos angled at "I'm into you." The body language was loud and clear.

"Lindsay, you're very pretty," The Englishman declared in that accent every woman swoons over. And let's keep it real, that accent has the power to make our panties drop.

"Can you please say that again?" I asked without skipping a beat.

We shared a laugh. Where was The Englishman my last night in Japan when I felt so pretty and alone, the butt of jokes at a wine bar? He would have been the perfect companion, sipping on wines from all over the world before engaging in hot sex upon the tatami matted floor of my room!

"I play guitar," he informed me.

"*Really*? I have a guitar at home!

"Yeah?"

"It needs some tuning, but yeah!" I responded.

He played soccer. I've always found soccer bodies the hottest of all athletes. So I became excited about my new fantasy of a musically inclined English soccer player serenading me with more than just his voice.

The date ended on my living room floor, and he did play a string instrument. At one point, we shared a sensual, down-tempo duet to The Beatles' "Here Comes the Sun."

No, we did not have sex, but my pants somehow ended up around my ankles. It was shortly after that point, I weakly protested. It was time for him to go. I was not going to fuck this guy on the first date.

It was bad enough I'd gone against one of my serious first date rules and invited him back to my place. I usually don't budge on that one.

He continued gently kissing my nether regions after I protested. It wasn't easy to resist his advances, but somewhere in between his caresses and his own objections to my objection, I saw Mr. Baby Crazy's face. *Fuck. No.* I knew it was going to take the familiar arms of Mr. East Coast to not see that face again. Why the hell was I even thinking about either of these men while an attractive Englishman and I were engaging in foreplay?

A few weeks after a couple of failed, albeit half-assed, attempts at seeing The Englishman again, he texted me that he was "tied up" for the weekend. He was spending time with a friend in town from London. I told him it wasn't a problem because I, too, had plans.

Maybe when I return from New York, you can tie me up. (*Insert winking face emoji*).

Naturally, he liked the sound of that, and while it may have happened in my imagination during a masturbation session or two, it never happened in real life. Neither of us made an effort after that, and I have no idea why other than that he was a rebound.

He could have ended up being a good fuck buddy though I think there are rules to having a fuck buddy: knowing the person well and sharing some connection, for starters. There has to be a level of trust involved, or it just becomes a one-night or a few nights stand, in my humble, horny opinion. The only hope I ever had in online date #8 was his potential to be a fabulously delicious rebound. If ever there were an ideal rebound, an Englishman who sings and plays guitar and tells you you're very pretty in his sexy English accent would be it, though. What sane woman wouldn't allow her pants to hug her ankles after that?

I began craving sexual connection with someone, more so than usual. I felt sexually neglected like my so-called prime years were wasting away. Horny all the time, I was like a *pubescent boy,* or perhaps, worse. Someone could ask if I'd like some nuts, as in a bag of Planters salted honey roasted peanuts, and my mind would automatically go to some hot guy's nut sack. Sometimes, I'd even put a face to the owner of said testicles, eventually imagining myself sitting on said owner's face. A few times, admittedly, that face belonged to James - my very attractive, close male friend. You know, the one Mr. Baby Crazy confessed his jealousy of?

Around this time, I began sharing the details of my dating shenanigans with James more frequently, albeit in very watered-down terms. He'd been online dating and sharing with me, as well, seeking the female opinion. I appreciated the male input. I, however, did not share the part where his face was often the owner of the aforementioned testicles.

Masturbating wavered between feeling like this spiritual, transcending moment of feminine power to a profoundly emotional and tear-ridden reminder that *I'm alone*. Sometimes, it almost felt masochistic in nature, though always serving as temporary relief. That conversation with myself, my therapist, or my closest confidantes consisted of how sometimes we know how to physically please ourselves better than anyone else. However, the truth is that it's just not the same as when someone is doing it for you. A man's tongue is far superior to a smooth, piece of vibrating plastic. There are probably exceptions. No scratch that. There are *definitely* exceptions to this rule. If sexual chemistry is non-existent or the other person is just no good in bed, then I'll take my hand or a vibrator over that shit any day.

One day, I arrived home to find that maintenance had entered my apartment to fix the clogged shower and the ceiling fan in my bedroom. What I didn't realize until later, though, was that I'd left my sex toy right next to my bed. *Lovely*. I'm sure the maintenance man enjoyed the sight of a hot pink dildo lying on the carpeted floor with the morning's leftover juices still lingering on its tip. Hopefully, he didn't get close enough to see those details, but still.

Sure, I could have picked up the phone, texted The Englishman, and asked, "What's up?" I could have possibly been in his bed less than an hour later, but I'd only spent a few hours with the guy.

"You're very pretty" became a daily, repeated inside joke between a friend and me. We began using it to praise one another, complete with our very best British accents, always rendering a mutual laugh while serving to build one another up. This friend also became my number one supporter in getting me laid. Her suggestion was consistently the same gentleman and mutual friend.

"What about James?"

She was met with the same response every time, which often sounded similar to not wanting to fuck up a six-year friendship for a good lay or two. If I allowed James and I to happen, Mr. Baby Crazy would also be right. Maybe there *were* sparks between us, and the only people in the world who didn't realize it were the two people creating them. But I wasn't ready to let Mr. Baby Crazy be right about anything – especially that.

James and Mr. Baby Crazy aside, I'll be forever grateful for the few hours I spent with The Englishman, who had no qualms about coming over, sitting on my living room floor, and playing guitar. I despise unnecessary acronyms, so I will spell it all out – You Only Live Once. Unless every bone in your body is protesting, in other words, your instincts say otherwise, let that man come over, play your instruments, and serenade you! Hell, let him pull your pants down around your ankles before you kick him out. You'll never regret it.

HOPE IS A BUSY FATHERFUCKER

I couldn't rid myself of hope, which led me to wonder if this was supposed to be my life? What if I was meant to live a life of endless dating, getting my hopes up, and ultimately being disappointed because that's all I know? What if I'll subconsciously always make sure I never succeed at getting what I deserve and what I've felt like I've always wanted? What if I'm destined to self-sabotage for my lifetime? I.e., choose a man who is unavailable in one way or another.

I once told a childhood friend of mine, Ryan, that hope is such a funny thing, but with all the shit I've been through, it's sometimes all I've got.

"Sometimes, it's all you need." His response couldn't have been truer or more needed at the time.

Such torment were the nights I lied awake waiting for David to return home from a night of partying only to discover he was passed out drunk on the Q train riding back and forth from Coney Island to the Upper West Side. Synonymous were all the nights my dad was mine and my older brother's sole guardian because my mother worked late. Guardian is a stretch when you consider that he was passed out on the couch, drunk and high.

David and I attempted marriage therapy prior to our ultimate demise. By this time, we'd moved to Los Angeles. Three years after very high highs and devastatingly low lows, I decided to extract myself from the marriage. Lying fetal position on the floor of our guest bedroom in the dark one night, I realized that no matter how much I love someone, Patti Smyth and Don Henley were right. *Sometimes love just ain't enough.* Unfortunately, there was no breaking through David's alcohol problem or his self-diagnosed personality disorder that would sometimes leave him rejecting me beyond repair.

"I think I made a mistake," David said to me, one night, after one of our frequent fights, five months after our wedding day. "I shouldn't have married you. I'm only going to hurt you," He continued rattling off a barrage of shocking statements, seemingly disconnected from all reality. His bleak, brown eyes stared off into the distance instead of at me before he made the most alarming of all his declarations, "I don't know if I love you."

My heart tumbled to the torrid pits of what hell must feel like. Those are not words one can simply dismiss or easily bounce back from. It reminded me of the time my dad told my mother and me how he felt about us during one of his drug binges.

"You fucking cunts. I hate you both."

I was sixteen years old when I became familiar with heartbreak, when I developed a disdain for whoever made up the whole sticks and stones bullshit. Words hurt, especially when they came from the first man I craved acceptance and love from. *Especially* when they came from the man I married.

So, fatherfucker was the word my feminist friend and I coined one day while questioning why motherfucker was the chosen derogatory term. Why were mothers, women, *females*, the only ones being fucked? So, yeah, we took it there.

It was easy to point fingers and place blame on the likes of my dad and David, but it wasn't making me feel any better. I'd been reflecting on so much in the aftermath of Mr. Baby Crazy and me when I asked my therapist if one just ever gives up on love.

"I fear becoming that person who is so jaded that she doesn't try anymore" I admitted to her.

"I think people become numb." She said.

The thought of becoming numb frightened me even further. Numbness is something I never wish to experience where love is concerned. Numbness is far worse than making a conscious and jaded decision to stop seeking love out of our disenchanted, hopeful hearts.

One afternoon, I was sitting at the bar of my local Whole Foods writing this very book you're reading right now when two young, twenty-something men sat down next to me.

"It's like politics, girlfriends, and feelings and political correctness. It's all too much for me, man, *like leave me alone*!" I overheard one of the men say to the other.

I almost spat out my rosé and shouted, "That's fuckin' life, buddy!"

I started noticing complacency with a lack of emotion in so many of the human interactions I was encountering, and not just the dates. I find it quite sad that so many folks would rather not feel deep emotions, wading in the shallow waters of self-medication and superficial feelings. Their knack for maintaining a routine of temporary relief appears like permanence, creating a false sense of reality. To imagine all of the potential connections that are being missed is of great despair, driving my own inclination to self-medicate and throw in the towel. But, I'm stronger than that, or perhaps my heart and desire and *hope* for something deeper, *something better*, is strong. I learned early on that many would rather pop a pill than put down the shovel. Perhaps my drive to *not* become that masochistic fool, slowly digging toward her grave was stronger than the occasional urge to surrender.

TO-GO OR NOT TO-GO

Pro Dating Tip: If he takes the to-go box, he's a no-go.

Online date #9 and I met at an Echo Park bar that Mr. Baby Crazy and I had gone to before a Dodger game. It was the same bar where I found out his obsession with making it to three months of dating one person was widespread knowledge.

When my slightly short, though good-looking date with the crooked smile and dark olive skin ordered a non-alcoholic Arnold Palmer, I felt strange ordering a glass of wine, so I stuck with water. When I mentioned this to friends, I was questioned why I had a problem with his beverage choice. Honestly, there was nothing wrong with him ordering an iced tea and lemonade concoction, but I was instantly uncomfortable. Maybe this says more about me than him, but this date didn't seem to be going anywhere except perhaps an AA meeting.

Over our PG drinks and a shared margherita pizza that we barely touched, I learned that Arnold Palmer had a roommate who worked at the same company and in the same department as The Englishman. I became suspicious. Was I being tested or set up? Or was this an "it's a small world" type of situation? *Or* did the roommate actually know about my pants around my ankles date? *Or* was the roommate The Englishman? (*Insert inquisitive, thinking emoji here*). Perhaps this was all just paranoia but the coincidences were uncanny. Not to mention, I don't even believe in coincidences.

I sat through an hour and a half of Arnold Palmer's elitist travel experiences and mind-numbing love for cars while consuming mediocre pizza without much acknowledgment or conversation about my hobbies and likes. I, too, like to travel Arnold, but you wouldn't know that because you're too busy bragging about that time you flew in a private jet and how you could never see yourself sitting in coach again. (*Insert eye-rolling emoji here*). I was *bored*. I don't get bored.

When he eventually asked for a to-go box, I was grateful to be going. He failed to ask if I'd like to take any pizza home, for the record. Arnold Palmer ordering and split entrees aside, if you have the ability to bore me, there is *not* going to be a second date. In the famous words of my favorite movie character, Forrest Gump, "That's all I have to say about that."

HEY, BEAUTIFUL

Pro Dating Tip: If he tells you he *was* a narcissist, he probably *is* a narcissist.

He was waiting for me outside Glendale's Din Tai Fung, a Chinese dumpling restaurant chain. Clad in hipster attire and nerdy, black-rimmed glasses, I was instantly attracted. Thankfully, there was no man bun, but in its place, a noticeable cowlick. I can relate. The tattoos aided in the attraction level, as did the intellectually stimulating conversation consistent with our initial connection via Coffee Meets Bagel. We discussed everything from art to music to politics, travel, and science.

First judgment told me that this guy took himself very seriously, sprinkling moments of humor into appropriate intermissions. After seafood dumplings, the thirty-three-year-old Taiwanese American suggested continuing our date over libations. I agreed. I didn't mind the spontaneity. In fact, I welcomed it, given my desire to go against the familiar grain.

We happened upon a new venue dubbed "Pussycat Lounge," complete with live Austin Powers reenactments. It was here he kissed me at the end of a busy, loud bar. He was quite a good kisser, and I definitely wanted to see him again. The night concluded with me giving him a ride home since he'd arrived at our date in an Uber.

The following week at work, my cell lit up with a text message before noon:

Can't wait to walk around naked with you in Spain…drinking wine…so romantic.

If a guy says this to you after date number one (awkward pause), I'm supposed to offer up some sort of sage advice here, but, honestly, I got nothing. I got nothing but heart on the sleeve and butterflies and cheese, er with that wine. Ugh, you'd think I would have learned by now. Maybe it's that I don't want to learn. If I'm completely honest with myself, perhaps I like the thought of walking around a Spain flat, naked with a stranger, consuming copious amounts of vino.

With that being said, let's discuss the importance of being honest with ourselves. There's something in being vulnerable with an audience, but the genuine, valuable growth lies in being able to look in the mirror and tell the person looking back at you the dark, embarrassing, or uncomfortable truth. If my tenth online date had asked me to move to Spain with him for a month or so, I would have seriously considered it!

Our second date was a few days later. He set it up, which scored him major points. The planner in me always appreciates when someone else takes the initiative. It was a Thursday night, and we met at the Sayer's Club in Hollywood. Over a couple of drinks, many laughs, and an in-depth conversation about our past, I learned about his narcissistic history.

"I used to be very self-involved, but I've been working on that with my therapist," he confessed.

I took mental note of this. While commendable that he sought the benefits of a therapist, this didn't mean there weren't still traces of his self-proclaimed narcissism hiding in the shadows. I was proud of my acute awareness and ability to not just sweep it under the rug as I initially did with my ex-husband's love for booze. He's young, and youngsters like to party. This is what I told myself when we met. I was twenty-five, and he was twenty-one.

I drove Mr. Narcissist home again and, this time, I went into his place. Against my better judgment, we fucked that night. If I'm being honest, which, let's face it, is pretty much what this entire book is about, or I don't think you'd be interested in reading it, I don't think I was judging at all. I guess I'd checked self-judgment somewhere between fucking The Doctor on the first date and being sexually attracted to a man that wears glasses for aesthetics and rolls the cuffs of his jeans above his ankles. Yep, definitely not judging myself if I desired to see what was underneath that denim.

The sex was as okay as I feel with a low-grade fever, which probably felt more like great sex for my neglected, feverish nether regions. I didn't spend the night. In fact, I left shortly after we finished our little romp in the sheets upon what resembled a couch's pullout bed. I noticed my leaving after fucking him resulted in a distinct feeling of power and self-control, unlike the morning I woke up in The Doctor's Tempur-Pedic® bed.

Mr. Narcissist texted me one workday afternoon, a couple days post fucking:

Hey, beautiful.

I thought about how powerful those two words are for a woman, or at least for me. They're two little words that go a long way. Every time I thought about that message, I smiled for the rest of the day. The thought that he could very well be greeting every girl he's dating with the exact same flattery did not turn my smile upside down. It also did not render me naïve.

We went to see the latest horror flick of the summer, A Quiet Place, on our third date. We met at Universal Studios' AMC theaters. Our day date was only slightly awkward until he proceeded to hide underneath his denim jacket for a large portion of the movie. Then, it was really awkward. Wasn't that supposed to be me? Okay, maybe that's sexist of me. It didn't actually bother me at the time, but I wasn't about to throw my arm around him or anything. I imagine if

I'd covered my face as much as he did during that film, I'd want my money back.

While on vacation in New York City during Memorial Day weekend, Mr. Narcissist's birthday passed. I picked him out a cute card at one of my favorite bookstores to hand-deliver upon my return. But let's keep it real, I was scarcely thinking of him while in the attentive and passionate company of Mr. East Coast.*

I spoke to Mr. Narcissist a couple of times while in New York City, once briefly during a girl's night out my last night there. I'd bought tickets to a rooftop movie in downtown LA, and thus our fourth date was planned. A few days after my return, we met on the corner of Olive and 9th to watch *Coming to America* on the rooftop of an apartment complex. We didn't stay for the whole movie before we made our way to The Golden Gopher.

I silently followed suit and ordered a Moscow mule à la The Doctor. Had it not been for my very first online date ever, I may never have known that consuming alcohol at a downtown Los Angeles staple could be such a charitable occasion! That, and I may never have realized how much I enjoy having my toes sucked on while

---

*Don't worry, this visit with Mr. East Coast gets its own chapter later. Patience, my friends.

being fucked. (*Insert cliché "everything happens for a reason" remark here*).

"I need to say something." Mr. Narcissist began.

That was a daunting way to begin a conversation, I thought.

Let me just paint the picture for you really quick. The Golden Gopher was *packed*. We'd scored the last two stools at the very end of the bar while the Friday night after work crowd swarmed in around us. Drinks were being poured, and the music blared when Mr. Narcissist proceeded to tell me that he wanted to take things "slower." He explained that he had a tendency to "jump into things," and he was trying to "do things differently."

The do things differently part, I understood. The taking things slower part was a tad confusing. After some coaxing for clarity, he explained he didn't want to have sex just yet. Um, last I checked, we'd already crossed that bridge.

Post drinks, I gave him a ride home again as he'd again taken an Uber downtown. We agreed to meet that coming Sunday for an afternoon hike as we hugged goodbye in the front seat of my car. I wasn't going into his apartment again as he'd just made it clear that he didn't want to engage in sexual intercourse just yet. I know I was just as confused as you must be right now.

We both showed up to the hike, our fifth date, horridly hungover from separate outings the night before. Cursing every incline with pounding hearts and sweat bullets dripping down our temples, we laughingly wondered why we hadn't just gone for a greasy breakfast somewhere. We were proud of ourselves when we reached the summit of the Wisdom Tree hike in Hollywood. He pulled out his phone to begin taking snapshots of the gorgeous three-hundred-sixty-degree scenery. I offered to take a photo of him, the San Fernando Valley against a beautiful, clear blue sky in the background.

Some of our conversations revolved around strange past stories that painted him as the other guy that the boyfriends of his friends hated or shallow small talk about how he couldn't bear to get rid of HBO or Hulu to save money on bills, even though he had Showtime and Netflix. I was honestly *bored.* During this hungover hike, I began questioning whether or not I wanted to continue seeing Mr. Narcissist.

I offered to show him my place when we got back from the hike since I'd seen the inside of his place. What could possibly be the harm in that? This was date number five, and we were drenched in sweat, so it was safe. Besides, he wanted to take things slow, whatever the fuck that meant.

I was going to Orlando on a business trip that coming Tuesday, so we wouldn't see each other for almost two weeks. As I bid him goodbye in my living room, he grabbed me, one hand on the back of my sweaty neck and the other around my waist. He planted a very aggressive, very sensual kiss upon my lips, tongue lunging toward the back of my throat. This guy, who, less than forty-eight hours prior, had told me he wanted to take things slow, only came up for air to ask if I'd like to shower with him.

"No!" I stammered, "Yes, *No*!" I wavered between restraint and horniness. I wanted to, but no. This guy was a confusing tease. I pushed him away and told him to get out. He agreed that that was the best course of action. What in the actual fuck? After he left, I chained the door and showered *by myself* before pulling out my loyal, hot-pink, vibrating friend.

SELFIE ABSORBED

Posting a photo on your dating profile taken by the girl you're dating is never a good idea. It's even worse if your profession revolves around shooting video and photography. I know your fucking smartphone gallery has well over two handfuls of selfies – pick one, bitch! Or, at least give me some damn photo cred! (*Insert camera emoji @me, asshole!*)

I was walking around Florida's Disney Springs when I discovered that Mr. Narcissist posted the photo on his dating profile – the very same photo I'd taken of him at the summit of our hike. After sending him a screenshot of my findings without any words, he frantically asked to explain his faux pas. I made sure to enjoy a nightcap or three* before heading back to my hotel room to take that phone call.

"I honestly wasn't dating anyone else. I know this sounds corny, but I think you're an amazing person. I appreciate you hearing me out."

---

*It was three.

"Are you just a quantity over quality type of person?" I asked out of sheer curiosity.

In allowing him to further explain, he offered up what I already knew:

A. He wasn't thinking of me when he posted the photo.

B. He's still a narcissist.

I assured him that I held no ill will toward him but that I had no intentions of ever seeing him again. Only the four walls of my hotel room could see how far in the back of my head my eyes rolled when he tried wishing me the best. What is with that? Don't wish me the best, fatherfucker! Wish you'd been my best. I should really write rap lyrics for Cardi B. Cardi, call me.

MY MOTHER SAYS HELLO

My head gently lay on Mr. East Coast's shoulder in the back of a taxi my first night in New York City. It was Memorial Day weekend, and we were en route to my downtown hotel after a night of dinner, drinks, and dancing.

"I'm so happy. This has been a wonderful night." I said with an audible sigh as the Manhattan and Brooklyn borough's city lights swam together in the dark reflection of the East River. I wanted to bottle up that feeling, savor it for the rest of my breathing days.

"Yes, it has," Mr. East Coast returned the sentiment, squeezing my hand that lay in his lap.

Several hours before, he'd walked into Esperanto, one of my favorite Latin Lower East Side restaurants, packed with six of my closest friends, and embraced me like we'd known each other for years.

"You look great!" He complimented me, his sexy, subtle accent making me feel like I was home.

"So do you! Thank you for coming!"

Over boozy caipirinhas, buoyant conversation, and a delicious meal, we all decided to go dancing at The Pyramid Club, a short walk from the restaurant. Mr. East Coast and I danced in the dark to eighties tunes. Our sweaty bodies glistened under the club lights, occasionally teasing one another with an arm rub here and a hip bump there.

While The Cure crooned, "Just Like Heaven," I leaned in close to Mr. East Coast, throwing my arms around his neck. My lips grazed his ear lobe as I said, "I can't wait to take you back to my hotel room and take a shower with you."

I pulled away just in time to view the big smile forming across his face that told me he, too, was looking forward to what lie ahead.

The taxi pulled up to my hotel. Three minutes later, Mr. East Coast's body was against mine, his lips against my mouth, in the corner of the elevator as we eagerly rode to the eleventh floor. When we finally entered my room, our damp clothes quickly came off before washing the night's grime away from our naked bodies. The shower steam, incessant groping, and tongue wrestling, eventually overheated the both of us before we decided to take it to the bed.

We made love for the first time since that past November, though the familiarity was indicative in the way his arms cradled my body and the sensual touch of his mouth against my neck. As he filled me up with himself, I moaned, profoundly struck by the sensation that our souls knew each other. We'd been here many times before we were even cognizant.

We spent the next few days together, hand in hand, arm in arm. I wondered what life would be like with Mr. East Coast? Would the idea and verbal suggestion of permanence, of commitment ruin all we had? Would it fuck up whatever it was between us? Would it make him less a part of "the pattern" if we didn't acknowledge any permanence? Was he a part of "the pattern" at all?

The truth was that it always led back to the fundamental factor that Mr. East Coast was *afraid of commitment*. So why was I even asking myself questions that required commitment? I think it was because I knew that even though he was afraid, that didn't necessarily mean he didn't want it. At that point of otherwise failed relationships, I was certainly willing to give it a shot if he was. But I stopped short, reminding myself that I knew better than to think that I, or my love, could change a man. Been there, tried that.

As fucked up as it sounds, I came to believe that knowing he was afraid of commitment was also a part of the appeal. If two people could care about each other as much as we did without ever committing, then we had nothing to lose. Of course, there were exceptions to that sentiment, but what sane person, given both of our experiences, wouldn't gravitate toward the parts of that idea that were plausible?

During the course of five days and four nights, Mr. East Coast met and hung out with some of my closest friends, who eventually, no doubt, gave their seal of approval. He and I shared a bed, cuddled into the cloudy, late mornings, huddled near one another in coffee shops in the afternoons, and made love in the evenings. We shopped, dined, got caught in the rain with a single umbrella, sauntered through old cemeteries in Manhattan, enjoyed underground jazz over questionably clean glasses of red wine, and took tourist-centric pictures with the throngs of professional-camera-wielding travelers.

He was conversing in Spanish with his parents, who'd just called him from the Dominican Republic as we walked, arms intertwined, through an overcast Battery Park post downpour.

"My mother says hello."

"Hola!" I returned the greeting, surprised that his mother even knew who I was. *He told his mother about me*. What did this mean? It didn't take long to remind myself not to overthink it.

There's no more significant time that I feel the impact of my own fears of commitment than when I'm the subject of "meeting the parents" or other familial regalia (Re: "My mother says hello"). Mr. East Coast later explained that his mother played a significant role in his fear of commitment.

Shortly after his phone call, we reached our destination, the SeaGlass Carousel. It was unique with giant, colorful fish as the carriers, housed behind a glass enclosure overlooking the waterside and designed to conjure up an aquatic vibe. I wanted to ride it for two reasons: One, I love carousels, and two, my mother loved sea glass. She and I used to spend many an hour perusing the beige sands of the Pacific coast in search of the tiny, smooth, brilliantly colored glass hiding in the grains. I have jars of it scattered throughout my home, a constant reminder of the simple joys my mother found solace in. And who better to join me in the three-and-a-half-minute experience than the man who'd been bringing me so much joy for the last few days?

Memorial Day weekend 2018 in New York City was certainly one for the memory books. This was *happiness*. Why couldn't it last? I returned to Los Angeles with a stupid birthday card for Mr. Narcissist and a natural high uninfluenced by external substances. Dopamine ruled.

IN MEMORY OF EMOTIONALLY UNAVAILABLE MEN

Upon my return from that incredible weekend in New York City, I told a friend, "Mr. East Coast isn't an option. He's someone I have a strong connection with, and we have good sex and enjoy each other's company, but we will not be a couple living on opposite ends of the country."

I was only telling her this to make myself feel better about how I'd just spent four completely blissful days and nights with Mr. East Coast under the pretense that it would never go beyond that. It was a shame, and it was out of my control.

I think back to my statement now and realize I could have summarized what I was trying to say with, "I wish he wasn't afraid of commitment."

Later that night, a damp puddle formed on the carpet beneath my cheek while I tried stifling the sound of my uncontrollable sobs. Instead of slumber, I was curled up on the floor, struggling to breathe through a barrage of tears. I'd like to report that this was an isolated incident, but it was not. I reached for the phone to text or call someone, anyone, and I remembered that those "anyones" are all probably sleeping and/or sleeping next to someone; a person they can confide their worst fears to, the very fears that had me lying fetal position on my bedroom floor late at night.

Forty-four minutes shy of midnight became an opportune moment for my emotions to acknowledge the what-ifs and the emotional availability that Mr. East Coast lacked. In those vulnerable moments of intoxication, the plausibility of drunken texting became highly likely.

You're probably sleeping, but I'm awake and thinking about you. Just wanted you to know.

Life's shortness was palpable as I typed out those words. Mind you, it was 2:16 a.m. east coast time. The alcohol swimming in my bloodstream urged me to say more, but thankfully, some semblance of sober reasoning intervened. Reason, in fact, strongly protested.

Mr. East Coast was the closest I'd come to the kind of comfort I sought. The smartest thing to do would be to quit it all, right? *Fuck the twenty first dates with twenty different men*! But I knew it took two to tango, and he'd made it very clear from the moment we'd met that he wasn't into that dance.

The following morning, all of my inebriated actions came to the forefront of my mind. I was fortunate in that I didn't feel any regret about sending him that message. I knew I was honest. Communication has always been a priority of mine. The hard part lay in believing his feelings were mutual, but his fear so overwhelming, it wouldn't allow for anything to ever come to fruition.

Eight hours after my message was sent, he texted me back. It started with three smiley face emojis in a row, followed by:

I hope you're sleeping now mums.

Mums was a charming nickname he'd given to me in reference to my curves. He'd also mistaken the word "moans" for the daisy-like flower during a conversation we had one morning while lying naked in bed, his head on my breast, my arms draped over his neck.

That's it? I thought to myself. Repetitive emojis and a wish for my slumber? Why? Why did you have to come into my life and mean so much to me only to be unavailable? Years later, I got around to asking him that question, but I never received an answer which I suppose is an answer in and of itself.

I reached for the trinket he bought and sent to me for my birthday, and I began to weep. I wept because life didn't really make sense at that moment. Everything that made sense was in the palm of my hand, and a nickname typed out across my cell phone screen. Everything that made sense was a couple of time zones away and in the fifteen words of a candid, drunk text message. Why was I wasting my time with these "online" men when there was a perfectly good man for me out there? But, even in my brief, emotional meltdown amongst all of the why's and what-ifs and common sense, I understood I'd consciously be succumbing to "the pattern" if I pursued these feelings.

It may be what I know and what I'm drawn to, but I'd committed myself to actively pursuing something else, something *unfamiliar*. I'd been working too hard to throw it all away now, to settle for something I knew was unavailable. I knew I deserved better. Mr. East Coast wasn't a bad guy by any means. In fact, I can't say that about half the guys I've fallen for. These weren't bad men.* I just always needed the thing that most of them couldn't give me.

---

*Except for Man Child. He was a bad man. *Bullet dodged.*

THE ONE I GHOSTED

Pro Dating Tip: Ghosting is #LAME. Just be honest.

The thirty-six-year-old Filipino engineer with the bold, tribal tattoos up and down both arms casually asked if I wanted to get something while sipping on his half-consumed latte. I'd just joined him at Pie Hole in downtown Los Angeles' art district, and I was slightly late. Not fond of the meeting place, I agreed to meet him there anyhow. When online date #11 asked if I wanted to get something, he didn't make a move to stand up and get it for me or even join me in the long line. So I quickly stood up to fetch myself some tea.

As I've mentioned before, I'm not one of those women that need to have the man pay for everything. I consider myself an equal opportunity spender, but I instantly saw the lack of effort in this man. Call it instinct, call it woman's intuition – it's all the same, right? As I always reach for my wallet when the bill comes, I don't think it's too much to expect the man to at least offer to get me my goddamned four-dollar caffeinated beverage.

After a hardly tantalizing conversation over middling tea, he suggested we battle it out over some Mortal Kombat at the barcade a few blocks away. At this point, he did pay for my wine before I lost the game. I so wanted to win for his lack of effort at Pie Hole. Guys hate losing to girls. After Katana and Scorpion dueled, we went and sat on the patio where bar-goers' cigarette smoke unpleasantly infiltrated my nostrils and attire.

It was a beautiful evening, though I honestly couldn't wait to leave. Mr. Lack of Effort was a nice guy, but sometimes nice doesn't cut it. For the record, I wasn't having a horrible time. Between the cigarette smoke and lack of a connection, I guess I just knew that this wasn't *it*.

Did I fail to mention that he was also shorter than I? This means he lied on his dating profile because, yes, I read *everything* before swiping right. I was wearing low-heeled, open-toed shoes, and he was noticeably shorter. There was no flirting, no body language to read, no genuine interest being exchanged. However, he must have been interested because he tried setting up a second date.

I agreed to meet him for a hike a week later, wondering if I wasn't too hard on the guy. Maybe he was just nervous? Maybe I was being shallow? And quite frankly, hiking was an activity, something to do on the weekend. I do love hiking, after all!

He suggested meeting near his place on the west side. I typically don't mind driving in Los Angeles, but there are plenty of hikes in my neck of the woods, for God's sake! I said it before, but I'll say it again: the man should make more effort at the beginning of dating, to meet halfway or closer to the woman's home base. It's a matter of chivalry, and while I'm intensely independent, I still believe in courting and certain gender-based notions.

I canceled on the second date. I told Mr. Lack of Effort that I wasn't feeling well. At that time, I was nearing my trip to New York City, and I told him I'd reach out upon my return with zero intention of actually reaching out. He reached out a couple of times in the weeks following my return and I completely ghosted* him.

As I write this chapter and revisit this encounter, I feel a little immature. The ghosting thing is such a sensitive subject. I'm sitting here typing, asking myself why the fuck I didn't just text the guy that I wasn't interested? I suppose Mr. Sweat might have something to do with this. Remember how I tried keeping it real per Google's suggestion and wound up feeling like it was more than he deserved, more than necessary?

What is the middle ground, though? I'm still trying to figure this out. I felt some guilt because for all Mr. Lack of Effort knew, my plane crashed or something. He eventually gave up after a couple of attempts.

---

*Urban dictionary explains ghosting as when a person cuts off all communication with their friends or the person they're dating. This lack of communication includes, but is not limited to, text and social media.

GET OFF YOUR APP

I will never understand what motivates people to use online dating as a means of finding a pen pal. If I were looking for a goddamned pen pal, I'd start writing to prison inmates at the local penitentiary, not filling out my interests on Bumble. At least the conversation would be a lot more interesting than how he mowed his lawn and tended to his garden on a perfectly good Saturday that he reserved for domestic duties instead of taking me to lunch. Under normal circumstances, I would find such activity interesting if we'd actually met before. In fact, if I had a yard, I would have been tending to my garden instead of texting his ass.

In another instance, I had a full-on telephone conversation with a man in between text messaging. We continued texting back and forth for a week or so when I suggested that we meet.

Don't you think it's a little soon for that?

His response took me by surprise.

Um, no, I didn't. Hence, why I suggested it. Isn't that what we're fucking here for? I didn't respond like that, but now that I think about it, maybe I should have. I'd probably have a lot more interesting story to tell you than the one about how we just stopped chatting one day shortly after my suggestion.

In another instance, I began talking to this guy whose name couldn't have been his birth name because it was so odd. Who names their son Stocking? As in stocking stuffer! I wanted to ask him about it so badly, but I didn't want to come off rude. I figured I'd save that inquiry for a face-to-face conversation on a third date or something, but we never even made it to date one.

Another gentleman went to the lengths of calling me on the telephone and having a lackluster conversation amid a couple weeks of texting. After we hung up, we both texted each other how sexy the other's voice was. We may not have had much to talk about, but when he was talking, I liked his sensual voice, each syllable delivering a new sexy scenario to my horny, overactive imagination. It's interesting how someone's voice can really enhance his hotness or completely turn one off in Janice's case (remember the anesthesiologist?) The point is, I never met the guy, and shortly after our phone call, we ceased to communicate.

I'm not sure what was happening, what it was that didn't warrant continuing the conversation. If I had to guess, I'd infer that it had something to do with work-life balance just not allowing these men to follow through. These were men with legitimate careers (well, most of them *cough* Man Child), and I understand the imbalance that sometimes occurs, especially in this country. I began wondering if American culture was actively playing a part in my inability to land a solid connection. You know, that whole mentality that we have to work long, hard hours to ever amount to anything, an attitude that values workaholics over maintaining healthy balanced relationships with our loved ones?

Or, perhaps their options were so endless, they couldn't decide, nor did they want to, on one person. It's like going to a diner hungry and looking at a menu that's ten pages long, and three of those pages list every different kind of omelet you can imagine. Yes, I just likened myself to an egg dish typically consumed during breakfast hours.

I'm not entirely innocent in participating in this cultural behavior either. However, in my defense, I followed my instinct on most occasions. In one such case, I made plans to go play pool with a guy as a first date, and the week and a half leading up to it consisted of minimal chatting or getting to know each other and a lot of gifs. I'm talking "good morning" gifs with teddy bears and fucking animated rainbows – all from him. *What the fuck*? I'm a morning person, but I've never even met you, so please don't send me fucking cartoon images to wake up to until at least date number four, and even then, you better hope I've had my coffee. By the time our date rolled around, I canceled on him in the morning after opening a gif of Fuzzy Wuzzy and a smiling, personified sunshine.

Another guy made it very clear that he just wanted some pussy. I entertained the conversation for a bit because, well, he was hot, and it was during a time when I was particularly sexually deprived. In other words, I just wanted some D. He once texted me mid-afternoon with a brief description of what our first date could be like, followed by a steamy photo of the shadow of his figure behind a shower door, clearly aroused and well endowed. He offered to pick me up on his motorcycle, and then I guess the world would be our oyster? Or my clit would be his pearl? He was a bona fide Bad Boy, and I resisted. Please pat me on the back because that resistance was no easy feat.

Over a year later, Bad Boy unexpectedly popped up on an episode of *The Walking Dead* that I was watching before trying to connect with me via every social app I'm a member of.

@MotorcycleBadBoy requested to follow you.

Hard pass.

And that's not his actual Instagram handle, people, so don't go stalking whosever this might very well be. *I literally just made it up.*

The non-follow-through is one of the strangest things about the online dating experience. Like, hey, I swiped right because I obviously liked what I saw and read. So let's flirt inconsistently and never meet until one day soon, we never text each other again, or in Motorcycle Bad Boy's case, until you social media stalk me even though I rejected you. My world is not your oyster, baby.

Why were these men even on the dating apps if they didn't have the time or energy to invest in their personal life? I call this phenomenon Pixelated Passion – no relationship progression beyond the initial exchange. Sure, I could have followed up on more than a handful of these encounters, but suggesting meeting in person seems like a pretty straightforward follow-through. Am I right? Or, am I right?

However, I was certainly not going to chase anyone. This was part of the commitment I'd made to myself when I began dating anyone after Anthony. Life is too short. If I'm going to run after something, the man will have to either run with me, next to me, toward the winery, to the beach or away from the body we just buried together because, well, ride or die and all.

Some close friends of mine were simultaneously doing the online dating thing. We would share stories and many laughs over our encounters. For example, Ryan, that childhood friend of mine, went on a Bumble date with a strikingly beautiful woman that he swore "came right out of Wakanda!"

Ryan, a mid-thirties Black man from the Midwest, was ecstatic about his date. When they sat down at a bustling bar, she immediately said, "First off, I'm a Trump supporter. Let me tell you why."

"No need," Ryan cut her off, stood up, and left.

I couldn't blame him. I would have done the same thing. I frequently asked if potential suitors were Trump supporters before I even agreed to meet. But, hey, at least Ryan made it past pen pals! If the online dating apps did one positive thing, they accelerated the dating game.

In James' case, he once went on a date with a woman who texted him just as they were about to meet at a restaurant:

You're paying for dinner, right?

He still met her for dinner, and he still paid. It took a while for my mouth to close after his tale of the jaw-dropping audacity.

Let's talk about effort again. If you can't take the time to fill out your profile, what's to make me believe you're going to take the effort to maintain a relationship? In addition, if all of your answers and photos are funny without even a hint of seriousness, what's to make me believe that you're going to take a relationship seriously? If everything is a joke to you, then I must conclude that our relationship will be, too.

Here's a shortlist of some of the dating profile/dating app faux pas I ran into:

- A guy repeatedly spelled my name with an "E" even though it was clearly written across the screen in front of him: L-I-N-D-S-A-Y.
- A guy who ended his profile with "Let's taco 'bout it."

- A dude who once wrote that he was looking for "a woman who isn't going to act like she's interested one day then act like a bitch the next" right into his profile.*
- A handful of guys would initiate a conversation and then not respond to my response.
- A self-proclaimed "nerd other nerds want to be."
- A guy invited me to join him on a heist to steal Van Gogh's Starry Night from the MOMA. Apparently, he'd been "planning it for ten years."

I hesitated on swiping right on the taco guy since tacos are my favorite food. When I laughed and debated with my Very Pretty friend about this, she quipped, "He'll tell you you're pretty and feed you tacos." She knew me so well! Alas, I swiped left.

Call it deductive reasoning or just a means of weeding out the subpar from the superior or sifting through the crap to get to something real as my dear friend, Jacquie, put it. Jacquie was also dabbling in the online dating scene. She believed that we all get to a certain point where no one is going to "disturb our lives." Deep down, something innate in all of us will not allow any disruption, no matter

---

*Someone's been burned. I'm genuinely curious how many women actually chose to swipe right on that.

how attractive or promising. This was definitely some food for thought.

What will immediately eliminate someone from consideration for a first date? If their dating profile only has photos of them wearing sunglasses. I will swipe left faster than you can say "swipe right!"

Furthermore, I never allow any first dates to pick me up from my apartment. I meet potential suitors at the destination or damn near close, which I'm aware I've already relayed. The reason for this rule is that I don't want anyone knowing where I live if I'm not planning on spending substantial time with him. My address is reserved for someone I intend on seeing on more than a handful of occasions. Then and only then is he invited to spend time in my sanctuary. Yes, I know I went against this rule with The Englishman. No need to get all judgy about it.

I also had a go-to first date outfit: Dark American Eagle jeans, bell-sleeved Bohemian Free People patterned blouse with a deep V-neck and an open-toed strappy heel. It was just enough cleavage without going overboard or requiring frequent self-adjustments and just enough height so as not to tower over any dates who may have lied on their profile.

In addition, I had a pre-first date to-do list comprised of photos and details I sent to the same, two to five, female friends as follows:

- Pictures of me date-ready, about to head out the door (seeking the thumbs up emoji from the recipient or a gentle suggestion as to how to make my appearance better.)
- A screenshot of the guy's dating profile showing as much detail as possible.
- A screenshot of the Yelp page or Google Map where we'd be meeting. (One can never be too safe. If I never made it home, at least the bastard would be caught, and justice served – *hopefully*. I wonder how it feels to be able to date as a dude without these precautions?)

If nothing else, my online dating method made me more selective, rather than accepting invitations from the plethora of bottom feeders and succumbing to the whole "plenty of fish in the sea" sentiment that everyone's grandmother has been reiterating to them since their first adolescent bout with heartbreak.

TWO MEAL TONY

Pro Dating Tip: They're not always single.

I was speaking to Mr. Narcissist while I was ghosting Mr. Lack of Effort and sleeping with Mr. East Coast. And then came Two Meal Tony. I get it. I'm a little dizzy, too.

Our relationship began in South Korea. No, I wasn't in South Korea when I met him. However, he was there when he repeatedly pushed me to have an actual telephone conversation with him versus messaging through the dating app. When I say pushed, I'm not exaggerating. This man was adamant about connecting with me via telephone shortly after our initial dating app exchange. I interpreted his eagerness for someone sincerely looking for something genuine and long-term.

I appreciated this man's enthusiasm to communicate even though he was in another hemisphere. After a couple of days of bad timing due to the fifteen-hour time difference, we finally talked on the phone. He went so far as to reference our "future grandchildren" during our first telephone conversation as we discussed everything from what we're looking for in a mate to politics. Not-so-distant memories of Mr. Baby Crazy flashed through my mind.

This went on for three weeks. "Good morning sunshine," texts followed by filtered photos of him and his Korean buddies enjoying downtime between hours of hard work became the norm. He was in his late thirties, Filipino, shorter than average but, thankfully, taller than me, brown skin, and a dazzling smile framed in short, silky black hair.

Two Meal Tony was so excited upon returning to the States on the same day I returned to LA from NYC that he wanted to meet up the very next day. I declined his invite, citing laundry and exhaustion. I needed some downtime. So, we agreed to meet the following Saturday.

With fifteen minutes to spare, I parked half a block from the wine bar we planned to meet at. I never like to be the first to arrive, and though I don't know if "fashionably late" is a thing in the online dating world, it was indeed a thing in my world. My phone lit up with a disappointing text message from Two Meal Tony:

I need another hour. Sorry if this won't work for you - We can reschedule?

This annoyed the shit out of me. I was already there when I received this inconsiderate text. This was the same guy who couldn't wait to have a phone conversation with me, had been maintaining consistent communication for weeks, and tried meeting me the day after he got back from the other side of the world! Now, he supposedly needed another hour? If it weren't for the fact that my place was down the street, I would have told him we had to reschedule. It should also be noted that he didn't know my home was down the street, so the lack of consideration was not a good sign, but I agreed to meet him an hour later.

Two Meal Tony immediately gave off a trying-to-be-too-cool vibe. It's possible it was to compensate for the visible acne-scarred face that wasn't present in the excess of filtered photos he shared while overseas. Although it didn't bother me, I could see this as a type of catfishing.*

Somewhere around the second glass, he expressed his hunger. Not expecting this date to go beyond adult beverages, I suggested this great Korean fusion place down the street from my apartment. Of course, I left out the part about it being down the street from my apartment.

By the time our drinks were consumed and we headed to dinner, I wouldn't say I was excited, but I was genuinely curious. There was an air of fraudulence about Two Meal Tony's demeanor that didn't seem to mirror the man I'd gotten to know over the phone.

---

*Urban Dictionary defines "catfishing" as someone who pretends to be someone they're not, utilizing social media to create false identities. The goal of "catfishing" is usually to deceptively pursue online romances.

When the bill came for our wine, I reached for it, and he stopped me.

"I've got this. You can get dinner if you want."

Huh? I thought to myself. Did this man really just say I can pay for his dinner that wasn't even part of our first date plan? *Wow*. What a manipulative cheapskate! Internally rolling my eyes, we got into our respective cars, and he followed me the short drive to the restaurant. I was hungry too, so I decided I could put up with this guy's game over the short time it took to consume a meal.

At the restaurant, he behaved as if he'd been dating me a lot longer than a couple of hours. He was talking to the waiter like a long, lost buddy, motioning toward me, saying things like, "The lady here…" and other condescending quips, like, "The lady is always right." And then…*he ordered two entrees*. Not one, but *two*! This man grubbed on two full meals in front of me while I enjoyed a piece of grilled salmon over a bed of arugula.

When the bill came, I paid. I paid for *both* of his meals. *What in the actual fuck just happened*? That was definitely a first.

After dinner, we had one more drink at a bar across the street. He paid.

"I Googled you, Ms. Dellinger," he admitted, nonchalantly using my last name. Of course, I'd never divulged this type of personal information to Two Meal Tony. And I hadn't consumed that much alcohol to miss the sound of my father's surname rolling off his tongue like it had been in his mouth for a while, a longer while than that second meal lasted.

He didn't have a sexy accent to fall back on, either. If it weren't for my good ol' friend, *Benefit of the Doubt*, who, by this time felt like an unwelcome, degenerate third wheel, reminding me of this man's profession: IT security professional for a major corporation, I probably wouldn't have even considered a second date. And well, if I'm 100%, we all Google each other, right?

Two Meal Tony's overbearingness while in a different time zone and his tardiness while in the same time zone were symptomatic of his deceitful ways. His knowledge of my surname was the cherry on top of a cunning cake. He informed me that he was divorced and had no children, supposedly. Did I believe him on that front? Undecided. I even wondered if he knew I lived down the street, imagining his Googling went far beyond what my fucking surname is? Maybe *I* should have Googled *him*.

His attempt at a second date failed because he completely forgot he'd made one. He was all, "let's get together Thursday night," and after I agreed, Thursday came and went with no solid plans and zero communication. I can't make this up. The same man who borderline obnoxiously pressured me to have a phone conversation with him shortly after swiping right totally "forgot" he'd set up a second date.

When he texted me an entire week later, wondering how I was doing, I was very vague. His half-assed apology fell on deaf ears. I suspected that Two Meal Tony was probably two-timing women like he two-timed his dinners.

SEXTUAL HEALING

Pro Dating Tip: Good sexting should never excuse poor manners.

Lucky 13, I thought to myself as I drove toward Santa Monica for my thirteenth online date. Not only was 13 my favorite number, I was also about to gain some reprieve from the dry heat of summer in the valley. And if I was truly lucky, maybe I'd gain some reprieve from the dry spell between my thighs.

13 was tall, lanky, white, and handsome with a lush head of golden-brown locks and a charming snaggletooth that greeted me every time he smiled, which was often because he had a witty sense of humor. Our initial exchange had me laughing out loud on more than one occasion, so I was very much looking forward to the in-person comedy.

When he spoke, his Irish/English accent made the skin on the back of my neck flush. Or was that the coastal breeze and red blend I was drinking? I quite enjoyed the cockney inflections as much as he enjoyed what he repeatedly deemed my "sass." My impersonation of an English accent didn't impress 13, but it did impress The Englishman, so I decided this guy was just confused by his Irish half.

We bantered over a couple drinks at Santa Monica's Water Grill while the salty ocean air wafted through the softly lit, romantic bar. It was there I learned that he worked at the same company as Two Meal Tony (thankfully in different departments) and that an Englishman's cum apparently tastes like raspberries, the latter according to an online dating app troll* 13 once encountered.

By the end of the night, we ended up at his apartment that he shared with a roommate who wasn't home. It was a lovely west side bachelor pad, and he had a cat. The cat was decidedly an asshole because all cats like me, and this one did not. Now that I think about it, perhaps it wasn't so much that the cat didn't like me but more foreshadowing. The cat knew that even though 13 was my favorite number, this date wasn't so lucky after all. Don't sleep with him tonight. *Meow*. Do not take your clothes off. *Hiss*. I listened. We didn't sleep together. Although we heavily made out, my clothes did not come off. *Purr*?

For the next week or two, we made and canceled plans before I had to go away on the same business trip where I listened to Mr.

---

*The term troll, in case you aren't familiar with it, refers to someone in an online community who seeks to start quarrels or upset others using inflammatory, extraneous, or other disturbing tactics and/or language. In other words, a troll is an online amateur instigator.

Narcissist justify his dumbass decisions. Our sexting swiftly turned into what felt more like a verbal war of who could say the nastiest thing to the other at the most inappropriate time. Here's a little excerpt of some of the hot and heavy banter:

I think your pussy needs a good hard fuck.

On Date #3…maybe.

Looking forward to it.

You should be.

You're wet. I'm lying on my back rock hard. You could walk in, climb on me, pull your panties over and fuck me right now.

Aye…aye. Aye. I really like your imagination.

Good.

He was leaving on his own trip to Seattle upon my return from Orlando. During these fourteen days, give or take, the sexting wars continued.

I can't wait to find out if that Internet troll is right. Does an Englishman's cum taste like raspberries?

The following morning, while at Disney's headquarters for a business meeting, I passed my phone around to show my colleagues a photo. Unfortunately, 13 decided to continue our sexting wars from the night before while my phone was in the hands of the sales guy.

I wanna eat your pussy out underneath that conference table you're sitting at.

Fortunately, the preview of his explicit memo didn't include any raunchy context. *Thank God*.

One night while 13 was still in Seattle and clearly drunk, he sent me a photo of the space needle propositioning me with:

Wanna fuck up there?

Sure.

He then confessed his qualms with the fact that I'd been married. I sent him the thumbs up emoji. Whenever I send the thumbs-up emoji, it's usually because I have nothing to say because I'm angry. It's my passive-aggressive response and might as well be a middle finger.

Uh Oh, I've pissed you off.

I'm not emotionally invested enough to give a shit what an essential stranger thinks about my life choices of which he has absolutely no knowledge of.

And that was the honest truth. No skin off my back. Was I disappointed that we were never going to fuck after all of that sexual tension and aggression? No, because his stupid dick didn't deserve to meet my precious lady parts. Was I disappointed that my dry spell was going to continue? Yes.

Okay. Sorry for annoying you.

He cheaply responded.

I never heard from him again. I shed tears after the entire exchange was over, though not for the fact that there was no potential future with this person. I shed tears because it added fuel to the fear fire, the one where I was afraid this was going to be the status quo. I worried that everyone would be like him, and this was why I never wanted people to know I was married in the first place. How does one hide that sort of thing, though, without feeling like a fraud? Eventually, I came to the rightful conclusion that anyone who took issue with this part of my timeline or judged me in any way for it just wasn't for me. No need to hide anything.

I couldn't help but think about how much I missed unconditional love as the tears continued to cloud my vision, my mother coming to the forefront of my memories. I wondered if she had gone through anything like this in the aftermath of her divorce, feeling the onslaught of anger as I wished she were here for me the way I felt like I was always there for her. Anger was such a strange emotion when it came to the dead. When their death isn't a choice, how can we feel angry at their untimely absence? Well, I'm here to tell you, it's *real,* and *it's okay* to acknowledge those emotions.

THAT PROVINCIAL LIFE

I've had many a revelation throughout my dedication to my mental health. One of the most poignant was when I realized my dear, deceased mother, whom I usually had nothing bad to say about, was the root cause of quite a bit of my fucked-upness for lack of better terms. For starters, I watched her continue participating in a destructive relationship with my father for almost twenty-five years before throwing in the towel.

At fifteen years old, I was the one to resolutely ask, "*When are you going to divorce him*?" She told me, years later, that my asking her that one night during a quick escape to my aunt's home during one of my dad's drug binges was the moment she realized she had to end it. That's a heavy one even to this day. I wish I could have a conversation with her knowing what I know now that I didn't know then.

If I knew the things then that I know now when my brother judgmentally asked, "When are you going to find a good man, Linds?" I probably would have responded instead of hanging up and bursting into tears. In my impressionable early twenties, my brother's implication was more damaging than the failing relationship I was involved in.

Today, I'd respond to his question with, "I have a difficult time finding a good man because you and Dad never showed me what a good man looks like. Because I had to work so goddamned hard to teach myself what I deserve, to teach myself that *I am enough*."

However, I refuse to stand in the shadow of being a victim of the poor human relations that the first two most influential men in my life exhibited. No matter the childhood examples presented to me and the ideas implanted in my brain about all the good men being spoken for, I refused to believe that something else, *something better*, didn't exist. There had to be something *more* than that provincial life Belle so eloquently sang about during the opening scene of *Beauty and the Beast*...and I was going to find it.

A dear friend and former colleague reached out to me inquiring about my relationship status. I was happily and seriously involved with Mr. Baby Crazy, the last he knew. After briefly filling him in, he said something to me that meant more than he will probably ever know. Instead of delivering unsolicited advice, he texted me:

Whatever happened, I'm glad you aren't turned off to trying again.

It was effortlessly profound, a statement so simple yet more needed than *I* even knew at the time, and it was such a beautiful contrast to the rare relationship conversations I'd had with my own kin.

#KISSITANDQUITIT

Pro Dating Tip: A great kiss doesn't always turn that frog into a prince.

Damn, was my initial reaction to his dating profile picture. It was noon while lunching with some coworkers, and we were checking out the latest "bagels."* I showed his profile pic to my friends, who concurred with my shallow enthusiasm. One of them even preferred vaginas to penises, so that must say something, right?

Online date #14 was lined up on a Sunday evening after a Dodgers game I was going to with a group of friends, including James. To my disappointment, James and I didn't get the opportunity to converse much as ten other people surrounded us. I really wanted to tell him about 13. I wanted to know if women also got weird about a man who'd been married before. I wanted to feel less alone.

---

*Why are women the coffee and men the bagels? Is that some like "but first, coffee," ladies first bullshit?

After the game, I met the thirty-something cute lawyer with his big, dark eyes and fabulous smile in the hipster-ridden neighborhood of Highland Park at a busy bar called Block Party. We sat on the patio in the warm June evening watching beard-wielding, jean-cuff-rolling, non-prescription eyeglass wearing twenty-somethings play bocce ball and become inebriated off pitchers of "craft" beer. Did I mention how hipster everything was?

My online date arrived quite nervous, which I'm sure caused me to exhibit some of my own anxiety. He was small in build but not shorter than me. I didn't think I'd crush him in bed, at least. One has to discern these types of details. In fact, my discreet ogling presumed there was a lot of muscle to be revealed beneath the long sleeve polo tee and khaki slacks he wore. After one drink, we noticeably relaxed before the bouncer ushered everyone inside. The outdoor area was closed off for the remainder of the evening for some reason that can probably only be explained by a hipster.

We found a couple of seats at the blindingly lit bar and ordered a second round. We were obviously enjoying each other's company considering we kept drinking. *Anxiety: That, or he just wanted to forget that he was on an online date with someone he really wasn't that into*. If that were the case, though, it would take a lot more than blonde ale to remedy that ailment.

We shared a mutual love for photography and other forms of art, leaning in to speak in each other's ear at times as the crowd became denser, louder. The sound of his voice inches from my lobe delivered subtle, unexpected tingles down my spine toward my…well, self-explanatory. I was so horny. *All the time*.

After round three, he suggested we take a walk and get some fresh air. I obliged. Night had fallen, and it was one of those beautiful, cool summer nights in Los Angeles, the kind better spent outdoors inhaling LA's version of "fresh air."

We sauntered down a neighborhood sidewalk, lined on each side by beautiful craftsman-style homes while we continued the pleasant art-centric conversation. As we neared his car, he stopped and turned to face me. I felt his left hand catch my waist and gently pull me closer until his lips touched mine. We kissed. It was lovely and long, longer than any first kiss I can recall.

When we finally parted mouths, he offered to drive me back to my car since we'd walked quite a ways. As he pulled up to my car and I bid him good night, he leaned in for another kiss. This one was just as fervent and almost as long as the first. I figured this meant I would be seeing him again. We'd go on a second date and maybe kiss again, maybe even make it to second base. Wrong. I never heard from him again. In fact, he ghosted me, which is why he shall, henceforth, be known as #KISSITANDQUITIT.

FEARS AND OTHER HUMAN COMPLEXITIES

I began asking myself questions like:

"What if this experiment was more about discovering myself than dating twenty different strangers?

What do my choices so far in these men say about me?

Why date a man who desperately wants kids when I've had surgery to ensure I don't have them?

What does it say about me that I chose to continue dating a man clearly self-involved and more concerned with his appearance and social standing than what was going on on the inside?

What does it say about me that I engaged in highly charged sexting under the frustrating anticipation of acting out our fantasies?

What kinds of people am I allowing to infiltrate my orbit, and why does their presence feel like an invasion?

What kinds of thoughts am I allowing my energy to be utilized toward?

Are my daily actions serving me well or draining me?

Am I acting from a good place or out of ill will?

Am I self-sabotaging?

Am I giving the Benefit of the Doubt to undeserving individuals?"

I also began asking myself, perhaps the most important question of all:

"*What do I fear?*"

The answers were often confusing and contradictory. I tried to remember that we're all complex human beings and how Mr. Baby Crazy would often project his own complexities upon me.

The answer to what I feared was everything. I'm scared of it not working out. I'm scared of it working out. I'm scared of not getting what I want and what I deserve. I'm scared of actually getting what I want and what I deserve.

The fears and insecurities are a fuckin' mind fuck that, on the surface, makes no goddamned sense. However, what this fuckin' mind fuck shouldn't be confused with is a desire for it *not* to work out. I've always wanted it to work out. I want what I've deserved my whole life. *I fear it* because it's unfamiliar. That's all fear is, really - the hesitation that cohabits with the unknown.

Mr. Baby Crazy's mother's fear was that her son was going to die alone, to which I often thought, "Don't we all die alone?" I know what she means, but I can't say it's my greatest fear. The dying part is easy. It's the living alone part that's the hardest.

I fear being alone for the rest of my life. I've literally lost sleep overthinking how my ninety-year-old grandmother has lost three of her five children, her husband, siblings, and countless other family members, including her parents. Using a cane, she lives alone, and I can only imagine her daily emotional and physical grapple with the perils of loneliness. I've exchanged handwritten cards with her on this loneliness because I still believe in the soon-to-be-forgotten, impactful art of the tangible sentiment. I sometimes worry I'll end up exactly like her. I mean, we're strong women, but I want more. I want my life partner, my ride or die.

Humans, mugs, self-help books, and saved Pinterest quotes all tell me the same general thing: to follow my fears. The majority of my fear, when it comes to relationships, lies primarily in finding what I deserve one day, investing so much of myself into it, and then losing it. It takes a whole lot of self-awareness and energy to invest oneself into that kind of unfamiliarity, especially after experiencing so much loss at such a young age.

Look, I get it; nothing in life is guaranteed. Learning that nothing lasts forever was a discouraging, hope-slaughtering, horse pill.

"Forever and a day," my ex-husband, David, told me that was how long he was going to love me.

Two years after his bold declaration, his mother embroidered the sentiment in dark purple letters atop an ivory lace pillow that carried the rings on our wedding day. In fact, "Forever and a Day" was the entire theme of our ceremony while, perhaps, only a mere dream in our immature, inexperienced minds.

While his love lasted longer than a day, it certainly didn't last anywhere near forever. My hopeless romantic dreams of meeting "the one" at a grocery store and living happily ever after had since long been crushed somewhere between the time I stopped watching soap operas and embarked upon a lengthy divorce.

CATFISH STINKS

Pro ~~Dating~~ Life Tip: Don't always believe what you see on your smartphone's screen.

The only experience I had with catfish, before online dating, was when my father would cook it in our small apartment, and it stunk up the entire place. It pretty much tasted how it smelled, too. I'm still trying to figure out how catfish became the lingo for someone who appears very different in person than from his photos. I'm lost on that one. Someone, please enlighten me on this.

Catfish was online date #15. We started chatting for a couple of weeks before meeting, all while I was sexting with not-so-lucky 13. Catfish appeared fit and lean in all of his profile photos, catching my superficial eye with a picture of him in a baby blue tank top, showing off his bronzed squeeze-worthy biceps and perfect pearly whites. I could clearly see his kind eyes, and it didn't take me long to swipe right.

I had two tickets to see Questlove from The Roots, deejay at a downtown Los Angeles warehouse. Since I'd reached out to #KISSITANDQUITIT and been ghosted, I asked Catfish if he'd like to join me. Quite an unconventional first date, but what the hell? He happily and quickly obliged. We agreed to meet at the same barcade I battled Mr. Lack of Effort in Mortal Kombat.

Standing in the middle of the crowded half-outdoor bar at sundown, I was scanning the faces searching for the familiar smile and muscular tank-clad man from the dating app photo. I couldn't find him, but I did see a not so muscular arm fly up, waving in my direction. Squinting, I realized it was him, the only resemblance being the teeth out of a dentist's wet dream. We greeted one another with a friendly hug.

His profile photos must have been *years* old as this gentleman clearly had aged and gained some weight! It's interesting how I'm the one who ended up feeling like an asshole. Has anyone else ever felt this way after being catfished? I know my feelings were completely valid no matter how much compassion I might have for him or anyone else that plays this dishonorable game. Still, I felt shallow for being disappointed with his appearance. At the same time, I was deceived.

I've never understood why someone would want to do this. There is zero logic in falsely presenting oneself and expecting others to be okay with their expectations not being met. My first thought is: If he'll lie about his looks, or withhold information (in this case, the fact that he'd gained forty-five pounds or more), then what else is he willing to lie about or withhold?

As the initial treachery began to settle, I decided I'd kick his ass in some Mortal Kombat. That should ease some of my disappointment. That, and a glass of wine. I beat his ass with satisfaction *twice*, and I had a chilled glass of sauvignon blanc *twice*. I was feeling better already.

The thirty-six-year-old Mexican-American worked as a chemist, and photography was his hobby. He had an incredible eye for what made a great photograph, sharing a couple with me before our in-person introduction. In addition to our love for still imagery, we shared an enthusiasm for soccer and tasty food. With the World Cup just beginning, so many of our initial conversations consisted of who was playing whom, scores, and who we were rooting for.

His tendency to err on the side of *me, me, me,* however, was off-putting. Is this just nerves? At least he wasn't talking about sports cars or how he always takes direct first-class flights when he travels. However, Botox laboratories and shitty morning commutes aren't really my cup of tea, either. The excess of small talk was yawn-worthy. Not to mention, I wasn't physically attracted.

The most profound connection we stumbled upon was how we'd both lost our mothers. Alas, deceased parents don't always constitute a strong bond as we all process and handle grief differently. This didn't stop us from grooving on the dance floor a couple hours later while Questlove spun on the turntables. The fact that I could comfortably dance with him on a first date was definitely a plus. This would go down as a fun first and last date, if nothing else.

We briefly conversed on one occasion after our date, though neither one of us made much of an effort to see each other again. The conversation was full of small talk, and being that I'd made plans for our first date, I wasn't going to do so for the second one. It's actually kind of nice when things happen like this. We both knew there wasn't much more to explore, but we didn't need to talk about it or make things awkward. No one was being ghosted, and Google wasn't being consulted. It was simply two adults quietly, maturely going their separate ways.

LIKE A ROCK

Pro Dating Tip: Just because he's built like Hercules doesn't mean you're his Megara.

His dating profile stated that he was "built like an ox," and he wasn't exaggerating. His profile's body reference reminded me of that old Chevy commercial, "Like a Rock" by Bob Seger, while my horny imagination skipped right past the first date into those ox-like, rock-hard, *ahem*, arms.

He was handsome in his photos, but he was even more *handsome* in person. Did I mention he was handsome? Standing tall at six-foot-one, he had dark brown skin and big brown eyes. He showed up to my go-to neighborhood bar, The Red Door, well-dressed donning charcoal grey slacks and a tight-fitting white tee accentuating his muscular stature. Thank God it wasn't all looks. He worked in global logistics, which I couldn't possibly begin to explain, but suffice it to say, it was important and required shrewd brainpower, which made our encounter intellectually stimulating.

I offered to buy our first round of drinks, pulling the plastic out of my purse. He'd just driven over an hour from Huntington Beach to meet me. It was the least I could do, but the Ox insisted on paying.

It can be challenging to navigate the how-do-we-pay dynamics with an essential stranger during a first date. As I mentioned before, I'll always offer with intention. However, I gauge body language and verbal response, and I could see my offer didn't sit well with him. So, I backed off when his large hand pushed my plastic back toward its origins.

After finding a cozy corner away from the weekday crowd, we were able to talk about in-depth topics without it feeling awkward or like we should probably switch it up to something lighter. We spanned everything from physics to politics to race in four hours over two glasses of a delicious red blend.

Somewhere between sips of vino and a discussion about what it was currently like for a non-national Black man (he was originally from Nigeria) in America, he made it clear that the literal miles between us weren't an issue for him. I was surprised at his declaration. Driving to Orange County didn't appeal to me in the least, but if he was willing to make the trek, then I wasn't going to question it. I took his willingness to drive well over an hour to meet me as a good sign that we'd be seeing more of each other.

Could this be the one? And by the one, I didn't mean the one I was going to spend the rest of my life with. I meant the one date that would end this "experiment," and end up more than a mere distraction, the unfamiliar Knight in Shining Armor. Was The Ox going to conclude this journey and this book?

He was a devoted fan of Portos, the Cuban restaurant chain so many Angelenos boast about, shunning me for my eye roll at this restaurant's overhyped-ness. He did, however, strongly concur with my spiritual philosophy on how humans meet each other for a reason, so not all was lost. That was the compromise. He could enjoy his potato balls as long as we could philosophize the deeper reason behind our encounter. He also loved the churros at Disneyland, so at least we could happily consume fried dough covered in cinnamon together. I didn't have much of a heart to tell him I didn't care to go to overcrowded Disneyland, though. I figured I'd save that for the third date.

The Ox walked me to my vehicle like a perfect gentleman. It was there he wrapped those strong arms around my waist and went in for the kiss under a brisk, clear night sky. The kiss was memorable and welcomed. As we tongue-wrestled, I thought to myself how I couldn't wait to tell my friends about this date, the same friends who sent me thumbs-up emojis after I sent them pictures of my attire.

The Ox and I exchanged pleasantries the following morning. After a mutual laugh at my willingness to "try Portos once more," I never heard from him again. Thus, he went down as one of my "kiss it and quit its."[*]

My friends, including James, found my stories about my being kissed and never called back hilarious.

"Maybe you're not a great kisser," he quipped.

I begged to differ, but I can see why one might venture to assume that, and I couldn't help but laugh along. It had become quite the phenomenon. For the sake of material for this book, I wish I could ask each of these guys what the point was and actually receive honest answers. Nonetheless, I have to assume it probably had nothing to do with the kiss at all. I mean, I'm sure we've all been on dates with people who we're physically attracted to enough to kiss but otherwise not attracted to. Anything could've turned these guys off. Hell, it could have very well had nothing to do with me; instead, they're doing what so many of the people on these online dating apps tend to do – keeping their options open. (*Insert eye-rolling emoji here*).

I was just kissing the wrong men, I decided. In my opinion, it's one of the cons of online dating - that quantity over quality bullshit.

---

[*]I swear if a hashtag doesn't derive from this, I'll be sorely disappointed. A lot of anticlimactic saliva swapping went into the development of said hashtag, and there has to be some payoff!

It's perfect for a player or someone like Mr. Narcissist. Sure, I dated more than one guy simultaneously on a couple of occasions but only until I met one that was more of a match than the other. There's nothing wrong with that.

When my hairdresser was encouraging the online dating thing, I went into it thinking it's simple, right? We're all here for the same, or at the very least, similar reasons. We're looking for someone to regularly spend our time with, someone to sit in dark movie theaters with, enjoy meals with, fuck frequently, and call when we lock ourselves out of our apartment. I could probably write another book on all the various scenarios I've encountered that prove this theory wrong.

Truthfully, I don't have a problem with people who aren't looking for a commitment. If you want to play the field and never settle down, more power to you! If you want to date around, fuck around, and remain uncommitted, who am I to judge? What I do have a problem with is when people aren't honest about those intentions. Most dating apps clearly ask what you're looking for. If the app doesn't, the question is usually brought up during your first or second conversation after connecting.

If a gentleman said to me, "I'm looking to have a good time, but not interested in anything serious," I would be like, "Cool, okay. We're not going to be a good match, but good luck with that" sans judgment. I would then expect the same respect in return.

Unfortunately, I suspect most people aren't upfront about those types of things because of fear of judgment and/or a stronger desire to get laid than the integrity to be honest. In other words, they're just fucking assholes.

A DOZEN ROSES AND NO RAGRETS

Pro Dating Tip: If you're looking for a new wife, don't talk about your ex-wife.

A few days after The Ox and I had our great first and last kiss, I had my seventeenth online date scheduled with a gentleman I'd been speaking with for about a week. He worked in the industry of death. More specifically, he was the person that the loved ones of the deceased would speak to regarding the plot of land the deceased were about to be buried six feet under in. A divorced father of two young boys, he served in Iraq and was clearly not a stranger to the dark.

He was the only man I went on an online date with who had children. Children were never a deal-breaker for me. Would I prefer that the man I eventually end up with not have any kids? Perhaps that was true at one time, but I'd come to realize that that was an unrealistic expectation at this point in the dating game. I'm getting older, and it's unrealistic to expect everyone I'm interested in to not have children, ex-wives, or other baggage. And it could, in fact, work in my favor. A man who already had children could err on the side of not wanting any more. A man with children had already satiated the urge to spread his seed.

I once dated a guy (who I didn't meet online) who told me he didn't have any children. Three to four dates in, his close friend was the one who informed me that that was, in fact, not true. This guy had not one but two children. If he is capable of denying his own children, then he's pretty much capable of lying about everything else.

I once advised James to include that he had a teenage son on his dating profile. This way, he'd avoid the awkward "by the way" conversation during a date with a woman looking for her baby daddy. I just figured it best to go into a date knowing that this person has the most important details rather than be disappointed later when said person reveals their disdain for children. Sort of the way, I felt it essential to know if the person I was about to go on a date with was a Trump supporter or not.

I digress, however.

What if excluding men with children was a missed opportunity for true love?

"How do you think losing your parents has impacted your life both positive and negative?" he asked.

"Do you feel like fighting in a war has given you an advantage in dealing with grieving people in your day-to-day work?" I asked.

We conversed well into the early morning hours while the rest of the world was sleeping. Intrigued by his intellect, hardships, and willingness to share, I was looking forward to meeting in person. Not to mention, I've found that I relate better to people who have experienced some form of trauma.

I had my concerns, which included whether he was what so many of my friends and I deemed "thirsty," meaning he didn't care who he was dating so long as he was dating *someone*. The over-eagerness was noticeable. I thought maybe he'd pump the brakes in person even though he'd accelerated over the telephone. We both deserved, dare I say, her highness' name, *Benefit of the Doubt*.

Agreeing on a meeting spot for our date, he emerged from his car to greet me. I could immediately tell he was a lot skinnier than he looked in his photos. He was strong, though exceptionally lean. He went to open the passenger side door for me, and a dozen red roses were lying on the black leather seat. This was a charming, romantic gesture, but one rose would have sufficed. I didn't even expect one, but *a dozen*? He drove us to our destination.

"Can I hold your hand?" he nervously asked fifteen minutes into the drive.

"Sure," I held out the palm of my hand, though I felt like this was one of the, if not the most awkwardly forced, handholding moments in the history of dating. It made me realize how important small moments like that were. Holding his hand during that car ride didn't mean anything to me, nor did the roses mean anything. The only thing these gestures could suggest upon meeting someone less than an hour before is that one of us was trying too hard. When all was said and done, it felt somewhat insincere.

The consistent anecdotes about his ex-wife were a turn-off, as well. There was an apparent lack of confidence. This man was better than my pity, but I was also better than being the woman who had to remind him of his worth.

The date itself was slightly unconventional but totally up my alley. He'd packed my favorite food, fish tacos, for a picnic at Santa Monica Beach. This scored him major points since he'd obviously been listening during our foodie conversation at one in the morning.

Could it be? No! It can't be! Yep, it was! Oh, thank God he didn't see me! High Cheeks (remember, the vampire?), who lived nearby, passed us on his bicycle as we made our way down to the sand. I tried not to do the obvious double-take, and I'm pretty confident I did a brilliant job at discretion. That is to say, High Cheeks didn't see me.

I can only imagine how that introduction would have gone: *Hello, how are you? High Cheeks, meet the guy I'm on an online date with (*obviously using their actual names because monikers and anything else would just be rude and weird*). Um, I'm sorry I never called you or tried to schedule another date. I'm not really into forty-some-year-old vampires who prefer fucking women in their guest bedroom, but hey, I hope all is well.*

After the near-awkward encounter, we plopped ourselves down in the sand and opened a bottle of one of my favorite Trader Joe's wines. He gave our leftover tacos to a homeless man sleeping on the beach, which I admired. Dessert was blackberries, also one of my favorites and something he'd surprisingly never tried in his thirty-seven years of existence. I was delighted at his reaction to my favorite fruit as he first tasted its bittersweetness and the broad smile formed across his thrilled face. We cuddled near one another on the sand. It was summer, but it was chilly so close to the water.

"My goal is to make you fall in love with me," he boldly professed as we sat appreciating the sea at golden hour.

You may be wondering if any of these things were absolute deal breakers for me. At that point, they weren't. They were simply yellow flags. I definitely wasn't turned on, but I hadn't completely thrown in the towel. Sure, his brakes were pretty much non-existent, but at least I figured that out early on. All of this aside, he was kind and sweet. He was different from what I was accustomed to. I was actively trying to give attention to the types of men I wasn't immediately smitten with, behaviors and characteristics I was unfamiliar with. It was out of effort and hope in breaking the pattern of choosing a man like my father. I had no idea if it would work, but I didn't see the harm in trying.

Just because he came on a little too strong didn't mean I couldn't relay these thoughts to him. I considered that maybe my directness could motivate a different approach if things should progress.

Somewhere between fishing blackberry seeds out of our teeth and generous sips of red wine, the conversation proved to be a bit much. He repeated how his goal was to make me fall in love with him and confidently added, "It's only a matter of time." I needed this guy to know that the way to make any woman fall in love with him was *not* to consistently speak about his ex-wife or repeat that you're going to make her fall in love with you.

In one instance, he alluded to the fact that his ex was aware that he was on a date with me that evening, and he seemed too pleased with this. Up until that moment, I'd given him the *Benefit of the Doubt*. We all have a past and his certainly wasn't easy, but I realized these flags weren't yellow. They were sadly red.

I was soon informed that his wife was actually with us. Okay, maybe I'm being a bit dramatic. She wasn't actually *with* us, but her name was tattooed across his chest. I didn't want to see it. I immediately thought of that viral meme of the guy from the movie *We Are The Millers* with the "No Ragrets" tattoo. If you've never seen it, just type "no ragrets" into Google images.

"Why the fuck would you *not* have that covered up?" was, naturally, my first question.

If I recall correctly, his excuse had something to do with money.

The ex-wife's name tattooed on his chest was my last straw. This was where I'd drawn the line, er, in the sand. I would see this date to the end, but it was clear this man was still not over his ex. He had some personal work to do, and I wasn't going to wait around for that personal work to come to its fruition. I'd been working too goddamned hard on my own self to be ammo in someone's unresolved marital qualms.

After we finished the bottle of wine, we decided to walk around the promenade for a bit before making our way home. At one point, a couple of douchebags blatantly ogled me, and No Ragrets about had a fit. This inability to control his anger only assured me that I'd made the right decision. Was it rude of these assholes to deliberately stare and comment? Absolutely. But, if anyone should be offended, it was me. I attempted to divert his attention by grabbing his hand and commenting on the beautiful coastal weather. The last thing I needed that evening was a testosterone-fueled skirmish.

The roses unexpectedly lasted quite a while, a week, actually. And it was also a week later, he texted me in the morning:

There isn't going to be another date, is there? I put way too much pressure on you and this and made you uncomfortable. Rookie mistake as my therapist called it.

I'm afraid not. I think there are some unresolved issues with your ex, and you need to take time for yourself to get to a place conducive with being in a new relationship. I really like you as a person and enjoy our conversation. I hope that we can maintain that, at least.

I dropped the ball and got too excited after not having a decent date in so long, and I'm really sorry. Of course, we can still be friends, and who knows what the future holds.

I have to make myself very clear. Nothing between us will ever be more than platonic. I believe people meet for a reason. It can last a minute, an hour, a date, or a lifetime, but it's impactful and purposeful. The reason you and I met has nothing to do with romance, however.

Understood. The man that gets you one day will be very lucky.

I like to believe he's right.

A couple weeks had passed before No Ragrets asked me to meet him briefly after work. He had something to give me. I obliged on my way to therapy one evening, having no idea what to expect. I genuinely liked this person, and although I was slightly anxious about this meet-up, it was important to note that my instinct didn't warn against it. I pulled up to the Brand Library in Glendale, where he waited outside for me on the steps. He appeared like he'd just left a funeral, clearly coming from work, clad in a suit sans tie, jacket draped over his left arm, a mason jar in his right hand, and a book in the other.

We quickly hugged and exchanged cordial, friendly greetings. He handed me the jar. It was full of colorful sea glass, my mother's favorite. He told me that the story I'd shared with him about my mother's love for sea glass, our frequent hunts for it, and the unconditional love I shared with her resonated with him. He'd made a solo trip all the way to Northern California's Fort Bragg Glass beach to collect it.

With its silver lid, the jar was a quarter of the way full of various sizes of smooth, semi-opaque pieces of glass in hues of green, white, and amber. I thanked him, though I felt my words were insufficient in expressing the gratitude I was actually feeling.

With the jar in hand, I slowly walked to my car, feeling like I'd crossed an invisible threshold. I was enough. I am enough. *I have always been enough.*

After we parted ways, he texted me:

Look for the rock/sea glass shaped like a heart.

I was glad to be en route to therapy. I needed to talk about one of the sweetest, most thoughtful things anyone had ever done for me. I barely knew this man, and he didn't expect anything in return. Hoped for something maybe, but his hope certainly didn't belittle the grandest of gestures.

Clichés exist because they're true – One can never love someone the way he should if he doesn't love himself first. No Ragrets was still grieving the loss of his marriage and still learning how to love himself. I'd been there grieved that. We simply weren't on the same page, and we both understood that. One day, he'll make someone very happy, and someone will be very lucky to have him, too.

THE MOST EXPENSIVE FIRST DATE

Pro Dating Tip: Get your shit together before expecting others to be involved in said shit.

I was texting back and forth with the nineteenth impending online date while getting ready to go out and meet online date #18. Online date #19 and I'd been conversing via text and telephone for the better part of two weeks when I told him I was getting ready to meet a friend for dinner.

If I'm interrupting dinner with your friend, then please let me know. But if your friend is The Other Guy then let's keep talking.

This made me giggle because it was so something I would do. But, I never fessed up to the fact that my "friend" was, in fact, The Other Guy – *until now*.

That night, I met The Other Guy, a sexy, slightly shy native Peruvian, for a few glasses of wine at Idle Hour, a historic barrel-shaped bar in North Hollywood. He was a software analyst who spoke with a perfect American accent. I questioned why he didn't have an accent or pronounce his name the way someone whose first language is Spanish would. This appeared to make him uncomfortable. I ended up feeling like an asshole after he explained he'd been bullied for his lack of English upon arriving in America at the age of fifteen.

During the evening, the conversation carried itself as we took turns asking getting-to-know-you Q's. Thankfully, I managed not to ask any other questions that made me feel like a prick. I lost a friendly bet with him about baseball facts, which required me to buy the next round. Bet aside, I was more than happy to make amends for my earlier snafu.

The Other Guy was attentive though socially reserved. It didn't seem like he got out much. This might have been the case considering he told me he'd just recently started dating again after a couple of years of trying to get his "shit together." Admirable, I thought.

We chatted about my solo travels to Peru in 2016, bonding over the Peruvian game Sapo. The game's objective is to toss a coin in a toad figurine's mouth. It's not easy, but it's fun.

"You're really pleasant," The Other Guy interjected mid-conversation. It was a sincere statement though I wondered if pleasant is a good thing to be called on a first date? I'm still uncertain.

"Thank you. I like to think so?" I responded with an inflection that warranted a question mark at the end.

I learned about our mutual passion for writing, and, at one point, we briefly exchanged stories about the recent loss of our pets. This certainly struck a sensitive chord in The Other Guy's masculinity as he abruptly changed the subject. Was that a tear I saw forming in those beautiful, brown eyes?

Somewhere around beverage three, I found myself hoping for a second date as we flirted with our gaze. It was a school night, so we didn't stay out too late. He walked me to my car before confidently gripping me by the waist with one hand and pulling me toward his mouth. He kissed me more passionately than any of the twelve online dates that kissed me before him[*], his other hand entangled with the hair at my nape.

In between swapping spit and upper body groping, I realized his whole demure act was solely reserved for public situations. Had there been a bedroom and four walls at that moment, I wouldn't have recognized the man I just had a few glasses of wine over modest banter with.

I couldn't help but wonder, though, if this was going to be what seemed to have become the proverbial first date kiss, and that's it. The #kissitandquitit, if you recall? Would I never hear from The Other Guy again? He did just give me the most fervent kiss of any of my dates thus far. I mean, *this guy knew how to kiss*. At least there was that if this was going to be a #kissitandquitit kinda situation.

---

[*]I just had to count how many of the seventeen before him I actually kissed, and I was surprised to discover that it was a bit over 70% of the online dates I'd been on.

I discovered the fifty-eight-dollar parking ticket on my windshield after we parted lips, er ways. I'd parked in a loading zone, and I can blame Mr. Baby Crazy, the well-to-do-man who preferred I never pulled out my wallet and hated paying for parking. I guess I misunderstood him when he explained the dos and don'ts of parking in certain zones at certain times during one of our date nights in downtown Los Angeles where the parking situations are way more strict than in North Hollywood.

That ended up being the most expensive first date I've ever been on, what with losing a bet in addition to owing the city of Los Angeles. I should have taken that parking ticket as a sign, something along the lines of, "Don't Park your Life Here" or my favorite expression, don't place all of your eggs into this basket. What the hell does that even mean, by the way? Who the fuck ever made that expression up, and were they Easter egg hunting or some shit? Why wouldn't they want to put all the eggs into the same basket? Were there so many goddamned eggs it became too heavy? I'm good at digression when I'm uncomfortably acknowledging my sleeve's heart of boundless hope.

Maybe the key is finding someone who also wants to place all of his eggs into my basket but who also has trepidations because we'll be gentler with one another in that "I get you" kind of way. We'll understand one another without having to repeatedly talk about the why's or the what-ifs. Find someone who is also afraid of commitment and love but innately desires and seeks it. Hmm, Mr. East Coast may just fit that bill? *No, no, no*, that is not where my mind was supposed to go.

The Other Guy planned another date with me, and by that time, I'd officially gone on my first date with online date #19. The Other Guy completely dropped the ball under the assumption that I was upset based off a silly text message, and by dropping the ball, I mean he didn't follow through. The day he suggested we meet up passed, and I reached out a couple of days later with a watered-down version of "what the fuck?" I decided that I could get over whatever misunderstanding had happened after he assumed that our date was a no-go. Hadn't he ever heard that assumptions make us both donkeys?

I received random photos of him getting ready for work during the week when we'd casually text one another. You know, the proverbial selfie in the mirror, phone in hand kind? I wasn't impressed, nor did I care for the surface, small talk about his "busy" workday. Was he trying to get me to respond with a selfie of my own? Try harder, buddy.

Nineteen guys in, and I was proud of myself for never texting the wrong person. But, perhaps, I was a bit too cocky about my astuteness. When The Other Guy tried to set up the *second* attempt at a *second* date with me, Nineteen was texting me about *our* second date. I was multitasking at work, to boot, and I slipped and got the lines crossed.

Thursday sounds great. See you around 7.

I texted Nineteen. (*Insert palm to face emoji here*).

I think that was meant for The Other Guy you're dating.

What an asshole I am, I thought, as my forehead *literally* met the palm of my hand. I couldn't bring myself to tell Nineteen the truth. I'd only been on one date with him. It wasn't like I owed him anything. I did, however, feel bad lying about meeting my friend for yoga, which is the excuse I gave him.

The Other Guy's second attempt at a second date bombed again, not for anything I did wrong. I know, I know, everyone says that, right? Truthfully, though, I'm not sure what this guy's "game" was but making plans with me and not following through is a deal-breaker. It's even more of a deal-breaker in the beginning stages. Why would I waste my time giving that relationship a shot when he already wasted my time initiating a date?

A friend of mine tried giving him the *Benefit of the Doubt* in that maybe he forgot which day we'd agreed to meet.

LaChele, accurately replied, "If he old enough to ejaculate, he old enough to calculate."

I mean, *yep*.

Five days after the evening The Other Guy and I were supposed to have our second date that *didn't* happen, I received this text message from him:

Was thinking maybe we could start over. Maybe not lol. All good.

Um, what exactly are we starting over? And why the fuck was he laughing out loud about it? There was nothing to even restart. You don't get a redo. This isn't a fucking video game. And if it is, then this is Mortal Kombat and, I am *finished* with you.*

At least, technically, I only lied to Nineteen about going to yoga with a friend. In actuality, I just stayed home and probably wrote parts of this very book you're reading right now instead of going on a date with "The Other Guy."

I didn't respond to his inquiry for a do-over if you were wondering. I'd moved on, and Nineteen had something to do with this decision. At least The Other Guy wasn't going down in this book as one of my kiss it and quit its, rather one of the best first and last kisses. At least there was that.

---

*I didn't actually say that to him, though I kinda wish I had.

STARE WARS, EPISODE ONE

Pro Dating Tip: If it's going well, plan the second date while on the first one.

"What the fuck are you doing outside" were the first words I ever said to this man in person, setting the pace for the rest of our date. It was a triple-digit day in early July. Online date #19 awaited my semi-tardy arrival outside in the unbearable heat.

"Nice to meet you, too," He chuckled at my profanity and stood to hug me before we found a seat at a booth inside the air-conditioned bar.

Thirty minutes into our spicy, mixed drinks, I was hypnotized by the way his brown eyes smiled when I asked him to join me for date number two. I had tickets to the Dodger game that coming Friday night, and our first date was going so well, I figured why not? Much to my excitement, he agreed!

Nineteen and I walked to Starbucks, where we sat outside talking while drinking our non-alcoholic beverages intended to sober us up for our departure. The weather had finally decided to take half a chill pill while the conversation was effortless. We were laughing and people watching, discovering it was a favorite pastime of both of ours. As we tried to guess what sort of scenarios strangers were in, I asked him what he thought people would think of us if they watched us.

"Well, it definitely doesn't appear that we're on a first date. We're clearly comfortable with one another...and, I suppose we could be related, but that would just be weird. Plus, our obvious flirting suggests otherwise. Buuuut, we definitely haven't been together for a long time judging by our body language." He gestured toward the ample space between our respective places on the iron bench.

We shared a laugh, and I nodded my head at his very accurate assessment. After about an hour of warming a Culver City bench, people watching, and discussing how boredom wasn't an option in our lives, he asked if I'd like to get dinner. Nineteen had made it very clear that dinner was a first date no-no in his online dating practices.

"What if you don't want to spend any more time with a person past the forty-five minutes or so it takes to finish a beer?" he asked during our first telephone conversation.

I completely understood.

The sun was finally setting, and the significantly cooler air was a welcomed reprieve from the day's heatwave. Clearly wanting to spend more time together, we strolled down the street toward Tender Greens.

We ordered and chose to dine al fresco. Nineteen sat down across from me, less than two arm lengths away.

"Can I tell you something?" He asked between bites of his albacore salad.

Anytime a sentence begins with that, especially on a first date, I never know what to expect next. It could be extremely flattering, or it could be bizarre out of left field and unflattering. One never knows how to answer a question like that. Like, do I really want this guy to tell me something? Do I have something in my teeth? On my face? You're into orgies, and this is all a setup to gain my participation? I'm being *Punk'd*? I mean, the possibilities of what he wanted to tell me were endless!

We were, after all, having dinner, something this exceptionally attractive late-thirties professor and marketing professional adamantly declared he never did on a first date. But here we were, a few hours into what was supposed to just be a drink or two, date numero dos already set, and eating our first meal together.

I politely, albeit hesitantly, replied, "Yes, you can tell me something."

"You're a pleasant surprise."

And there was that word again – *pleasant*. I actually took it as the intended compliment it was because it occurred to me that "pleasant" is apparently rare these days. This label left me wondering what kinds of dates these guys were used to. Unpleasant? Did that say more about them or me? He further explained that he was surprised at how well our date was going and how down-to-earth I was.

During dinner, we made plans for additional libations while exchanging awkward dating stories. He won with the girl that told him, "It's all Gucci," in casual conversation. I didn't even fucking know what that meant, and he was relieved that a slang term overused in pop culture was not part of my vocabulary unless I was discussing the Italian luxury brand founded in 1921.

His eye contact was unfailing and intense between our getting-to-know-you chatter and heavy flirting. I returned the stare as much as my nerves could muster. In doing so, I couldn't help but notice the sexy mole directly below his right eye, the subtle crow's feet gently cradling it every time he smiled.

"Am I staring too much?" he asked with a serious but shy expression, failing to remove his eyes from mine.

I told him he wasn't, feeling a bit shy myself beneath his gaze. I searched for something to break the intensity and commented on his endearing mole. Modestly, he grinned, revealing something I hoped to get to know better. *I've never had a better first date in my entire life*, I thought as the STARE WARS continued.

After dinner, we walked across the street to a hotel bar where we cozied up on a comfy, velvet cushion in a dim nook of their upstairs lounge. Live jazz music carried its way from the ground floor dining room, much to the enjoyment of my ears. It was a lovely addition to the ambiance. He was obviously listening when I told him how much I love jazz.

"I know this is kind of a forward question for a first date, but," he disclaimed, pausing and tilting his head slightly right before asking, "What are you looking for?"

I begged to differ about the "forward" part encouraging him with how I thought it a perfectly appropriate and welcomed question.

"I'm looking for my ride or die," I confidently stated.

He chuckled. At first, I thought he was laughing at my idealistic declaration, feeling a slight sting of embarrassment. Perhaps "ride or die" was far-fetched and too ideal of a desire in today's modern dating world, or maybe it was something he just didn't believe in?

"That's the term I usually use – *ride or die*," he confessed, exposing that endearing grin again.

He was looking for the same thing. He wasn't laughing at me at all. The jazz music fell silent, and I heard absolutely no other voices from the lively crowd surrounding us. Time stood still as we locked eyes in a deeply romantic moment. It probably lasted a much shorter time than how long it felt. If he was thinking the same thing that I was, then we were both considering the genuine possibility that we were sitting across from each other's ride or die, or at the very least, *hoping* we were.

He broke the silence. "I want to know everything about you."

To think I almost swiped left on Nineteen because, in nearly all of his photos, he was wearing sunglasses! Thankfully, I swiped to the very last picture where he was sans sunglasses, selfie in the mirror, and donning suspenders over a white button-down, collared shirt with the sleeves rolled up to the elbow. I immediately liked what I saw. Well-dressed, fit, with soft, curly, brown disheveled hair, long enough to run my fingers through, and those caramel brown eyes. *Damn, those eyes.*

Before our official meeting, Nineteen expressed his desire to have an actual telephone conversation to "make sure there are no deal-breakers beforehand." I liked his approach. The conversation included everything from politics to religion, and I appreciated the candid, straight-to-the-point tactic.

"I can't date a woman who doesn't want a family," he stated.

I hesitated, feeling that familiar punch to the gut when Mr. Baby Crazy confessed his desire to be a father.

Taking a deep breath, I finally said, "I don't know if I want children, but I'm open to the possibility."

And that was the truth. If Mr. Baby Crazy did anything profound for me, it was my putting the possibility of children back on the table.

Now, over cocktails, we were diving a bit deeper into what ride or die meant for us on a personal level. I brought up my lack of ever wanting children. I even relayed how the prospect of having kids in a world where my mother didn't exist was the most significant factor in my non-desire.

"I'm open to the possibility of meeting the right person (AKA ride or die) and all of my reservations about having children becoming non-issues," I admitted.

His attention matched his declaration. He really did want to know everything about me. Nodding his head while I spoke and still staring into my eyes, he keenly noticed when the crowd became a bit overwhelming for my anxiety. I was grateful for his awareness as we took our leave.

Sauntering around Culver City just before midnight, partaking in some more bench-warming conversation, he opened up to me about some of his dark. His father was an alcoholic, and he was concerned about his own relationship with alcohol. In turn, I shared the long-story-short version of my father's battle with alcohol and pills. I realized a large part of the deep connection I was feeling with him had so much to do with his willingness to be vulnerable. His actions made me feel comfortable.

"I tend to be quite awkward at the end of dates, and I don't know how to act," he admitted, the mole under his right eye illuminated by the street lamp's glow.

I assured him that awkwardness was okay and that we didn't need to focus on the end anyway. We were sitting much closer than we were earlier before dinner. I think we could have watched the sunrise together if one of us had suggested it. But alas, the night came to an end. It was late as I drove him to his car. I pulled over to the curb, where we began bidding adieu.

"So, this is the awkward point I was talking about earlier..." He trailed off, "I'd like to kiss you, but I don't want to be too forward or make you uncomfortable."

Instinctively, I reached over and gently placed my hand on his forearm.

"I would like for you to kiss me," I confirmed.

We both leaned in. His coarse facial hair scraped the top of my lip as our mouths met.

"Text me when you get home safe," he ordered.

"Likewise."

I smiled from ear to ear the entire way home. Eight hours since asking him what the fuck he was doing outside, I could positively state that it was by far the longest and *best* first date I'd ever been on. In fact, those were the exact words I used when my friend, James, asked me how my date went.

DON'T FUCK THINGS UP, THEY SAID.

During the six long days after our epic first date and before our second date, Nineteen* and I texted often and chatted on the phone one evening. Friday couldn't come fast enough. I couldn't wait to see him again! I found myself placing all of my eggs into Nineteen's basket then tentatively removing one or two when thoughts of the last basket I carried around infiltrated my initially blindsided, hearts-in-the-eyes-emoji behavior. Yes, I was still on the dating app, though I wasn't actively talking to anyone.

I brushed up on John Mayer's catalog since discovering he, too, was Nineteen's favorite musician. I came across one song I'd never heard (probably because it was off of what many deem his "country" album that I wasn't an immediate fan of). This song described my feelings to a "T," so much so that I wondered if I'd written it! Nineteen was curious about the song and why it profoundly resonated with me.

---

*Number Nineteen is being called Nineteen for more than just because he was the nineteenth online date. Numbers and dates have always held a very special, primal place in my life. And this particular one was relevant in so many ways. Keep reading, and you'll understand why.

"Alexa, play 'In the Blood' by John Mayer," he commanded his smart speaker.

We listened to the entire song in complete silence over the phone. To describe what a beautiful four minutes and four seconds it was for me wouldn't do it justice. It was a you-had-to-be-there kind of moment, that kind of moment I'll never forget for as long as I live. And this is the part, dear reader, where I incite, no, I implore you, to listen to the song before reading any further.

A few days later, we watched our Los Angeles Dodgers (#spoileralert) beat the Los Angeles Angels on Friday, July 13th, 2018. I was having so much fun over booze, pretzels, Dodger dogs, flirting, and friendly banter.

While drinking in the club member's lounge before finding our seats, I was sweaty and felt like a hot mess. Literally – it was ninety-plus degrees that day. Nineteen reassured me that I looked "great" while simultaneously placing his hand on my back to better understand the sweat I kept complaining about. We both had a good laugh at just how sweaty I actually was. Not only was it hot as hell, but the second-date nerves were adding to my body temperature.

"So, that John Mayer song is pretty self-explanatory. Not much to be misconstrued there, am I right?" he asked.

"Pretty much." I concurred.

I think this was one of the first moments he really saw me. And by saw me, I mean he understood something about me that didn't require words or explanation. His attention and interest in detail were very attractive. Rarely, I feel genuinely seen by anyone.

An hour or so into the Friday, the 13th game, we were thirteen (my favorite number) rows behind home plate when he unexpectedly grabbed my hand.

"I was curious if it'd be uncomfortable to hold your hand with all the rings you wear." He said.

"You just want to hold my hand." I sang in Beatles melodic fashion.

His charming grin rendered my assumption accurate. Don't worry. He wasn't trying to get me to remove my jewelry before introducing me to his family. He'd commented on how he liked my style and jewelry, so his interest was genuine.

"It's not uncomfortable at all," he exclaimed with delight, our fingers intertwined as I silently prayed for my palms to remain dry.

It was the bottom of the fifth inning. My swamp ass thankfully went away in the nightfall while the alcohol happily swam through our veins. I'd just returned from fetching Nineteen a surprise dessert for his self-proclaimed sweet tooth. His appreciative expression warmed my heart as I hoped to be seeing much more of his face.

"We should probably see more of each other," he said between bites of his ice cream sandwich.

Could he read my mind?

"I think we should probably see more of each other, too." I casually agreed.

"My family told me not to fuck things up when I told them we were going on a second date," Nineteen said.

"Are you prone to fucking things up?" I asked.

"No, no, not at all. I just haven't been on a second date in five years."

My jaw dropped open, and I quickly closed it before he noticed.

"So, what could I do to fuck this up?" He jokingly asked around the seventh-inning stretch. I paused, wondering whether or not he was subconsciously trying to fuck it up.

"I don't know, and I don't really want to figure it out," I told him. He agreed as we laughed it off and changed the subject.

Nineteen was engaged twice in his thirty-six years of life, the second engagement having ended five years prior. Even though he exercised vulnerability with me, which I very much appreciated, I was beginning to notice hints of the proverbial wall he'd built somewhere in between engagement number one and engagement number two. There was a firm foundation, extra reinforcement, and plenty of insulation. It wasn't going to be easy getting in, but I knew with every fiber of my being that if I did, the interior would be beautiful. I'd experienced glimpses of it, peeked through the windows. I like to think I may have even shattered a pane or two. I mean, he was, after all, *on a second date with me*.

After the Dodgers won and we oohed and aahed at the fireworks display, he drove us to a downtown brewery in LA's art district. It was there, I discovered that we were both so good at taking care of ourselves and putting on our game face that no one was really worried about either of us. We actually wanted people to care, though, maybe even worry sometimes.

"Don't fuck it up, they say, but no one's even reached out to me to ask how it's going!" He scoffed, picking up his phone and dropping it on the bar for emphasis.

"I totally get it." And I did.

Finding someone who'd been harboring his own darkness, who had the capacity and strength to shine a light on whatever darkness I brought to the table, was refreshing. When people are willing to take off the mask to reveal something not so pretty and exhibit vulnerability in your company, acknowledge it gently and hold on fiercely.

My "I totally get it" was casual when, inside, it was in *italics*. There was *prominence*, an explosion of internal mutual sympathy, and the figurative shouting from the rooftops.

I totally get it, Nineteen!

Our date concluded with making out in the front seat of his Mustang while he introduced me to a genre of music he'd recently gotten into. It was sexy, instrumental mood music, and a great soundtrack to the tongue wrestling. After our lengthy make-out session, he drove me back to my car parked at Union Station. He got out to hug and kiss me one more time, my hands cradling his bearded cheeks.

I wore a smile the entire way home – another excellent, epic, eight-hour date with Nineteen was in the books.*

I started wondering if I would make it to online date #20. What if Nineteen was going to be my happy ending, only it wasn't going to end? Damn, this book just turned into a fairytale! *Shut up, Linds*.

I'm a living, breathing quandary of hopeful, masochistic, romantic, hopeless, realistic idealism. In other words, often, I feel like a nut. Sometimes, I don't. Scratch that - *rarely*, I don't.

---

*no pun, intended – *seriously*.

B SIDES

The following weekend, I drove to the South Bay where I met Nineteen at his apartment. It was my first time seeing his place, and I was impressed. Clean and nicely decorated, I very much liked his choice of modern art, complete with a black and white portrait of Audrey Hepburn hanging over a small corner office setup in the living room. An authentic, distressed cowboy hat draped over a coat rack carried past stories of an old roommate, and bookends made out of Edison bulbs lit the way for conversation topics. His bathroom was neat and adorned with amber patchouli-smelling candles and freshly laundered towels. The toilet seat was down. (*Insert clapping hands emoji here*).

We spontaneously drove to Redondo Beach pier for dinner. His idea.

Nineteen and I sat across from each other, sipping Mai Tais at Tony's on the Pier while watching the very active beach and birdlife when we weren't having an involuntary staring contest.

His stares often caused me to ask him, "what?" I don't know what it is, but I've always had issues with staring, even when I knew it was a positive act. If someone is staring at me, I automatically become insecure. Like, do I have a booger hanging out of my nose? Are you noticing how pronounced my overbite is?

Truthfully, I didn't want him to stop staring. His eyes were so engaging, a forest I hoped full of evergreens. The mole and that crooked smile always drew me in. At the same time, I admired other parts of him - his hands and his arms, especially the fresh tattoo on his right bicep, a kaleidoscope so beautiful with its intricate, fine black lines. However, my favorite body art of his resembled a mountain range spanning half of his forearm. The thin, long line called to me the way the mountains called to John Muir. It was simple yet striking.

I couldn't help notice Nineteen's nerves that seemed to mirror my own while I simultaneously imagined running my fingers through his wavy hair.

Asking one another what the other is thinking became a norm. He was the first person I'd met that didn't seem to have an issue with telling me what he was thinking. He insisted, like I, that "nothing" was never a legitimate response. I attributed this to our shared, overthinking, and complex minds.

"We're always thinking about something," he stated.

Mid meal, I excused myself to the restroom before pulling out my cell to let my girlfriends know how well our third date was going.

No Ragrets had texted me:

I just wanted to tell you thank you for making me realize my underlying issues. You were completely right about why people cross paths.

You don't need to thank me for this.

I do need to thank you. I didn't realize what I was doing. You were the only person that was willing to tell me. I don't want to interrupt the rest of your night. I hope you stay a beautiful person inside and out. Good night and sweet dreams.

It was the kind of thing we all wanted to hear. I helped someone realize something that would hopefully benefit him in the future. He deserved to be happy. If I could take credit for any part of that, then this endeavor to date twenty different men I met online was so much more than a challenge accepted and an entertaining story. And I could never forget that No Ragrets had given me something - the unfamiliar feeling of being *enough*.

I returned to the table where Nineteen was patiently waiting for me. We were discussing the abundance of birdlife and my overcooked salmon when I attempted to take a closer look outside at a particularly brazen seagull. I banged my head on the spotless glass window. Nineteen paused in shock for half a second before shaking his head and sharing a hearty laugh with me over the accident.

After our seafood dinner, we walked along the beach, getting caught in a wave, dampening the bottoms of our jeans. It was here, our toes in the sand and the sunshine permeating our exposed skin, that I told him I'd like to see him more often than once a week.

This seemed to trigger a nerve. Nineteen's face scrunched up underneath his sunglasses as his gaze fled mine for the first time that evening, for the first time since we'd met, really.

"I feel bad for being here, having such a great time with you," he confessed.

"Why?"

"I'm usually spending time with my nephew or helping my brother out with this or that. I'm the go-to for any help that's needed in my family."

It became clear that this man had become so good at taking care of everyone else's needs before his own. It was his routine, and it was his safe place, a familiarity. So, I decided I'd proceed with caution and a hopeful heart.

Feelings of guilt aside, we continued having a great time and watched the sunset from a brewery on the pier. It was apparent that this date would go down as another eight-hour marathon. Between sips of pilsner and admiring expressions at the pink and orange hues before us, he told me about his aunt's 80th surprise birthday party that he was planning solo.

"I was wondering if you would you like to be my plus one?" He asked.

I hesitated in my response. Meeting family was a huge deal for me, and he knew this. I was surprised at his invitation, being that we'd only been on three dates. Not to mention, the declaration he'd made just an hour before was still weighing heavy.

"Take your time in giving me an answer. I realize it's soon." Nineteen continued.

His eyes were as sincere as the invitation that escaped the mouth I couldn't wait to kiss again. When I considered that this man was going out on a limb asking me to come to such an important event, I decided I had to meet him halfway.

"I'd be happy to be your plus one," I replied with sincerity.

He returned a smile, and we finished our beers, sharing and giggling over past dating stories. He confessed that he'd ghosted a couple of women before asking if I'd ever ghosted anyone. I told him I had.

"Can I ask you to never do that to me? If you should decide that *this*, *us*, is a no-go, just be upfront, please?" I requested.

"I wouldn't do that to you. I think our relationship has reached a point where ghosting would be inappropriate."

I was relieved he agreed while noting his usage of the word "relationship" to myself.

When we got back to his place, I changed my saltwater-soiled clothes. He popped open a bottle of wine he'd intentionally saved for us before we lay on the couch for hours. Sharing music and conversing over John Mayer's B-sides, I was beyond content.

"Play 'Tracing.'" I insisted.

He was impressed that I even knew the song.

"My favorite line in the song is when he says, 'don't you know there is a reason strong moves slow,'" I told him.

He agreed with the profundity of that line.

My heart's desire for Nineteen to be my ride or die deepened while I lay my head comfortably in his lap, and he stroked the hair behind my ear. He did so without knowing how much I loved my hair being played with. Many a blissful time was spent in my mother's lap with her lulling me to sleep by this very same method.

We dissected every song played while simultaneously dissecting life.

I told him how John Mayer's "Heartbreak Warfare" reminded me of my marriage. I used to be the person who needed to fix everything at that moment rather than stepping away for a bit. But, I'd learned since that, sometimes, sleeping on things and walking away was just what was needed. He nodded in agreement, citing a similar anecdote from his last engagement.

From the perspective of his lap, I admired his coarse, dark beard hair against his olive skin and, once again, the mole underneath his right eye – *those eyes*.

He surprisingly broached the topic of the sex we had yet to engage in with one another.

"I just want you to know that it's not that I don't want to – *I do!* I'm just really enjoying getting to know you right now and taking things slow. I don't want to fuck things up."

"Thank you for telling me that. I'm not in a hurry," I replied, "I've been enjoying getting to know you, as well."

I appreciated his candor and willingness to acknowledge not-so-easy topics while wondering what he was so worried about fucking up. After all, there's a reason strong moves slow.

The hours ticked by, and the music played on.

"You've got to hear Childish Gambino's cover of Tamia's 'So Into You,'" he said eagerly, searching for the song on his phone.

I don't know if this song was his way of telling me how he was feeling at that moment, but that's how I took it. And the feeling was mutual.

Sometime around midnight, he joked, "We've officially spent an entire day together since our first three dates have been eight hours each."

He walked me to my car, where we hugged and kissed goodbye. I drove home, again, with the biggest smile on my face listening to John Mayer at full volume. Third smile is a charm? *Who was I*? I was getting to know a side of myself I didn't know existed, and she was as cheesy as French imported Brie!

Could Nineteen really be the lucky one given the last eighteen duds? Could I really meet the love of my life online? I wasn't even sure if I believed in such a thing as the love of our lives. I definitely didn't believe in luck, so that one got tossed out the window real fast.

"I think I've met the man I'm supposed to be with," I confessed to my therapist. It was a week after accepting Nineteen's invitation to be his plus one at his aunt's eightieth birthday party. I immediately followed this up with all the reasons why I shouldn't be professing that. What I should have been saying was, "I *hope* I've met the man I'm supposed to be with." I couldn't let every prior experience and lesson be overlooked by having these feelings so soon. If I'm being honest, though, what's the difference between thinking it and allowing the thoughts to verbally escape?

Cue my therapist and her psychoanalytic wisdom, "It's hope versus your prior experiences." *Yep. Touché.*

WADE AWHILE

Ron Howard dined an arm's length away from us at an obscure, lovely new restaurant in old town Burbank. It was a Thursday night, and Nineteen had just made a grueling bitch of a trek from the South Bay to the valley. I couldn't believe the immense anxiety I was experiencing while choosing the restaurant for our fourth date. I wanted everything to be perfect, especially since he'd just spent two hours in his car.

Nineteen was a movie buff, even dabbling in some of his own filmmaking. While the hammered bronze cutlery, speakeasy, old-fashioned tea towels, and exposed, industrial-esque piping impressed us, the fact that an award-winning director was dining next to us was exceptionally impressive to him. Nineteen once won an award for a thirty-second, Spanish language short film he'd entered into a contest. He'd written it, acted in it, and composed the music for it – that was impressive to me.

The almost full moon shone its lovely face over the low-rise retro buildings as we enjoyed our delicious dinner, sampling each other's dish. My anxieties about picking the perfect place washed away. In contrast, his anxiety about being "back in the valley" was an unexpected guest at the dining table.

Ex-fiancé number two resided in the valley, and he explained how he was the one to make that drive almost *every single day*. I immediately felt terrible, like I'd inadvertently opened up a wound that hadn't quite healed. He insisted that that wasn't the case. We discussed how much we both have a tendency to overthink *everything* because we don't want to make the same mistakes.

"So, basically, we're just two really fucked up people with control issues," he quipped.

I laughingly agreed with his deduction while remembering the things that make me laugh are sometimes the very things that make me cry.

I grabbed his hand amidst the melancholy, and he returned the gesture by squeezing mine. We sat there staring at our hands wrapped around each other for about sixty seconds before he broke the silence.

"You're one of the deepest people I know." He declared with what sounded like a hint of unease.

"Yeah, that usually intimidated the men I've been with in the past," I responded with transparency.

"I'm not gonna lie, I've thought about that." He admitted.

I knew what he meant, but it wasn't a conversation I was ready to prolong. I knew he was thinking about whether or not he wanted to swim or stick to the shallow end where he'd become so comfortable for the past five years since his last engagement was called off. The shallow waters were a much safer place than the depths at which my ocean went. I hoped he'd dive in and tread there with me awhile because from where I was wading, it was quite beautiful, and that acknowledgment, I realized, was not only growth but also self-love.

The part of me that was falling for him also hoped that I could become the big, bad wolf needed to huff and puff his walls down. So, I continued holding his hand while the little girl inside me ran and hid somewhere.

HEY, NINETEEN

About a week after Ron Howard, I met Nineteen at his place. I left work slightly early to make the nearly two-hour journey south. Listening to John Mayer croon, "Love on the Weekend," on repeat, I couldn't wait to see Nineteen's handsome face. (*It is okay to insert eye-rolling emoji here – I know I've become a sap*).

Nineteen had been wanting to take me to one of his favorite bar/restaurants in Torrance since we'd met, knowing how much I loved live music and seafood.

"You've got to try their salmon! I think you'll love it," he said.

It was a beautiful, cool summer evening as we cruised, windows down, toward our fifth date dinner. He was pointing out familiar places from his childhood while sharing details about the planning of his aunt's birthday party.

He pulled into the parking lot of an unassuming, wooden building on a busy thoroughfare. The sign outside the restaurant with the salmon I had to try was aptly named *Hey 19*.

Whoa.

"You know what I find amazing about you?" Nineteen asked over bites of tartare and sips of his Coors Banquet beer. This was a question I was a little more eager to hear the answer to than the one he asked on our first date.

"What's that?"

"I forget that you've been married. I've dated divorced women before, and they tended to have a…"

"Chip on their shoulder," I finished his sentence.

"Well, yeah. They had quite a cynical outlook on life, especially relationships and men."

I nodded my head, listening as a solo jazz artist began playing saxophone a few feet away from our table.

"There's just this innocence about you," he continued, "And I trust you."

"Wow…Thank you for telling me that."

That was a first for me. Trusting someone is not easily come by, so I took that to heart. Furthermore, innocence? That's not something many could see in me. Sure, the little girl inside of me that never received the kind of love she so desperately craved comes out every now and then, but *innocence*? Maybe he sees something I don't, I thought. Maybe I, too, had some walls that needed to be huffed and puffed down? I thought back to his comment about me being one of the deepest people he knew and decided it took one to know one.

This date was a far cry from the bitter declarations of date #4, in which he wasn't sure if he was ready to dive so deep. No man had ever ventured to communicate that he trusted me so early on in a relationship. I'm not sure what Nineteen saw or what I might have shown him without being conscious.

As we exited the restaurant, golden hour was settling in. We stopped briefly to admire the sky's masterpiece before he opened the passenger side door of his car for me. I let out an audible sigh that spoke volumes of happiness.

"If you ever record music again, you have to cover one of my favorite songs. Let me play it for you."

He referred to my writing, recording, and performing around Los Angeles from 2007-2010. I quit it all after my mother was diagnosed with cancer in December 2010. The motivation was extinguished with the devastating news.

In the time it took to drive the short distance to the beach, we fell silent while intently listening to Jessie Ware's "Say You Love Me." Our frequency of sharing music became one of the things I loved most about our relationship. We didn't have to shush the other during the magical three to four minutes. It was an importance we both understood without having to explain.

The sun was on its way to meet the horizon when Jessie Ware's lyrics about not wanting to fall in love unless the other person also wanted to try permeated my heart. The lyrics were the perfect soundtrack to a relationship seemingly evolving against all odds – his upcoming busy two-job schedule and familial obligations and our mutually dark, complicated, overthinking minds.

We walked along the coast in Torrance, just north of Palos Verdes Estates, appreciating yet another stunning sunset and the company of a palpable, undeniable connection. The Pacific waves crashed into the shore, dancing with the dimming orange light as he slipped his right arm around my waist. This was bliss. As we made our way back to the car, I learned Nineteen often rode his self-made electric bike on that same path we were on. His abilities and varying hobbies never ceased to amaze me.

We aimlessly drove a few blocks east when he spotted a neon red sign for a wine bar. He pulled over, parked, and said, "Shall we?" As I placed coins in the parking meter, he walked up, grabbed my face, and passionately kissed me. I can't describe how much that public sidewalk kiss is engrained in me. If I knew a parking meter would become the site for a moment that I'll never forget, I might have stopped shunning meter maids a long time ago.

Inside, we sat at the bar and ordered two desserts because Nineteen's sweet tooth couldn't decide between the cannoli and the crème brulée. He had me pick out the wine since I was well versed in the beverage. I chose a Malbec for him and a red blend for myself. He liked it very much, which pleased me. Then, over a not-too-sweet Italian pastry á la mode, he opened up to me about how me and his car were the first nice things he'd done for himself in years. While I wasn't sure how I felt about being in the exact likeness as his mustang, a material, albeit pretty possession, I understood what he was saying.

"That's why I said you first," he chuckled, justifying successfully.

Every time he smiled, I wanted to touch the mole underneath his eye with my lips. The more he drank, the more he relayed. We were getting to know each other on a level I had yet to reach with any of the eighteen men I'd met online before him. We were meeting each other halfway. I couldn't wait to go back to his place and gain some privacy.

That night, we lay on his couch sharing music, both of us stretched out and squished against one another. He was on the edge of the sofa with his left arm resting on my waist while his head was propped up on his right arm. Sigur Rós was on the stereo.

Before we met in person, we learned that we were both at Sigur Rós' performance at the Hollywood Bowl in 2016. When he learned about my love for the Icelandic band, he texted:

You just got bumped up to coolest girl I know.

I felt like a schoolgirl as we made out on his couch to songs with names that I couldn't begin to pronounce. I reveled in every last touch as our hands eagerly discovered one another's clothed bodies. Five dates in, and we had yet to have sex! This was different and exciting, serving to further validate our connection.

I always thought I was hard on myself until I got to know Nineteen. This man was always putting others ahead of himself, and I silently vowed to put him first if he'd allow me to. I thought I'd finally met my match. We could be there for each other in ways no one before ever could because we understood things about each other that others before us couldn't.

Maybe I was getting a little ahead of myself, or maybe it was, once again, the vino happily swimming in my bloodstream. Either way, I was going to enjoy every ounce of it while it lasted – all the vino and all the feelings. My proceed-with-caution approach had disappeared with my quarters in the parking meter.

A PLACE TO STAY

Mr. East Coast texted me the following week to share the news that he'd finally found a new apartment in Brooklyn:

Now you have a place to stay when you come to New York.

I wanted so much more. What made Mr. East Coast think that I, too, was afraid of commitment? What made him think that I would always be available for short holiday weekends and non-committing rendezvous? Maybe he didn't. Perhaps I was reading too much into it, but perhaps I needed to. He meant no harm. That much, I knew. I also knew he was extending the hospitality since he voiced on more than one occasion how bad he felt for my staying in a hotel during Memorial Day. I allowed him to stay with me when he was in LA, and therefore, he thought it right to repay the favor. I understood the concern while assuring him there were no expectations.

I've never felt it necessary to be in a relationship, but having a companion in this life is so much more ideal than going it alone. I *wanted* a partner. It's nice to "have a place to stay," but at what point as adults do we stop pretending that a roof over our heads during a long holiday weekend is remotely close to the shared space, time, and lives that we truly desire with another human being? At what point do we stop letting fear firmly stand in the way of more than temporary, of greater than fleeting?

I knew that I wanted a partner in life, and I knew it to my core. Every time I'd found myself alone, I found myself longing for more. As much as we might say we like the single, unattached life, we're human.

I'm constantly reminded of standing in the quiet, stillness of Nara Park, gazing upon one of the most beautiful scenes I've ever laid eyes on. Something was missing, and that something was *someone*. We'll always crave companionship, even the commitment-phobic Mr. East Coasts of the world.

HALF OF HIS HEART

You can sleep over at my place Saturday night if you'd like.

Sounds great. See you then.

Nineteen invited me to his older brother's birthday gathering, making sure to let me know I was welcome to spend the night post-festivities. Of course, the proverbial butterflies fluttered their wings at the sight of his text message.

Meeting his brother was a big deal – at least it was for me. Nineteen sometimes had an annoying way of acting like very significant things weren't important even though he knew they were – that too-cool-for-school air.

"It's difficult for me to meet family members early on in a relationship," I told him on our second date.

"I understand, but you'll probably be seeing a lot of my brother. He's my best friend."

Leading up to the birthday party, I confided in James, who had several close siblings of his own. I asked him what I should bring even though I wasn't expected to bring anything. I couldn't show up to the party empty-handed, though. I couldn't meet one of the most important people in Nineteen's life for the first time without contributing in some way. James suggested a homemade mango salsa. I loved the idea, so mango salsa it was!

The Saturday morning of the party, I woke up early to shop for fresh ingredients. I made the salsa just before hitting the road, knowing the drive to the South Bay would take me well over an hour. Then, it would probably be another hour before we actually arrived at the party where his brother, sister-in-law, several of his cousins, and a large chunk of his closest friends were in attendance.

"I've heard so much about you," His brother approached me, "Scratch that, I've heard so many *great things* about you."

This instantly made me smile, and Nineteen witnessed the exchange from across the room while voluntarily mixing drinks for partygoers. We shared a mutual stare that lasted longer than the typical Stare de Nineteen. It made my heart feel like Apollo 11, and Nineteen's hands were the moon.

He sat down next to me later on in the evening.

"What were you and my brother talking about earlier?"

"Don't worry about it," I replied with a smirk.

He chuckled.

Throughout the evening, I'd spoken in great length with many of the people in attendance while Nineteen stole hesitant, sweet glances from the other side of the kitchen island. My salsa was a hit. Some dude even put some on top of his pizza. While this didn't sound particularly appetizing, it definitely stirred further interest and compliments. I genuinely liked Nineteen's circle, especially his brother, and I felt like I fit in.

As the night neared its end, the birthday cake was consumed while movie debates ensued, and I felt the excitement of what was about to happen creep in. I knew that when Nineteen and I left, I'd be going back to his place and I'd be sleeping in his bed. Inside, I was like a teenage boy about to lose his virginity. I knew that we were finally going to have sex.

When we got back to his place, it was well past midnight. It didn't take long for us to explore each other's bodies with fervent hands as soon as the lights went out. At last, we were naked while kisses were exchanged in places other than each other's mouths. Sigur Rós' ethereal sounds went unnoticed next to the obnoxious groan of the window unit air conditioner, which was louder than everything, except for my moans.

I didn't sleep well that night. I woke up wishing I'd been soberer for our first time. I wondered if this was why I didn't feel as connected to him in the morning light. We lay in bed for a bit before attempting morning sex. His man parts responded, and then they didn't.

"Wow, did I just go soft on you?" He nervously laughed, trying to ease a sensitive situation with humor.

I told him it wasn't a big deal as I casually rolled over, only slightly insecure. He rolled over with me, his arms wrapping around me tightly, his chin resting on the back of my neck, nose in my hair. Any insecurity I may have felt quickly disappeared with every one of his inhales. I hadn't felt this wonderful or been held like that in a long while. Basking in a comfortable bliss, I felt safe and warm. My proceed-with-caution flag was at half-mast, sort of like his boner.

"This feels so good," I said with an audible, relaxed sigh.

Seconds after my declaration, he abruptly released his embrace, ushering us to get up and get ready to go have breakfast. It reminded me of online date #2, The Lawyer, AKA Elephant Man when he jumped up and said he had to leave mid-conversation. At that moment, I went from feeling Nineteen's all to feeling his wall. I knew he felt good, too, and I knew it scared him.

Slightly hungover and very hungry, we dined outside at the Del Amo mall in Torrance. It was between bites of avocado toast and sipping on a mediocre Bloody Mary, Nineteen brought up his looming, hectic schedule.

He wanted me to advise if he should or should not take on the added work, divulging details of financial responsibilities I wasn't aware of before. He was given the opportunity to teach an extra college class, which meant twelve to fifteen-hour workdays three days a week. I didn't feel like it was my place to tell him how to live his life or conduct his dual career, but he pressed me for my input.

"Don't you already feel stretched with working two jobs as it is? Why would you want to take on the extra work when life isn't balanced, to begin with?" I paused, taking a sip of water to wash down the poor Bloody Mary aftertaste, "Plus, you're already worried that you're not devoting enough of your time to your family. This will only burden you more."

There. I gave him my opinion.

He didn't end up taking my advice, and I can't say I was surprised.

I knew he was telling me so much more than how busy he was about to be. What made the situation more difficult was the timing of when he was telling me. We'd just slept together for the first time literally hours before he made his upcoming lack of social life (i.e., time for me) public knowledge.

Do I think that he just wanted to fuck me? If that were the case, he wouldn't have waited over a month worth of dates to get me into his bed because I probably would have dropped my panties on our first date. I think we were becoming too close for his comfort. His taking on the added responsibility was a good way to physically avoid that closeness without being honest about it.

I was beginning to wonder if it was the Bloody Mary that tasted so bad or the situation I'd found myself in. Less than twenty-four hours earlier, we were stealing romantic glances across his brother's living room at each other, and I was getting to know his inner circle. Now I was being told that all of that would be a rare occurrence. I was crushed and pissed all at the same time, disguising my emotions with the symptoms of my hangover.

He asked me to another Dodger game the following evening. I assumed his invite was supposed to ease the blow of the previous declaration, like one last hoorah for old time's sake!

After work the next day, I met him at a bar in Union Station before the baseball game. He was already there, sipping a beer as I approached the table. I immediately sensed something was off. He seemed preoccupied and anxious, not exactly happy to see me. After I grabbed a glass of wine, I sat next to him, nervously consuming my red blend while wondering what was going through his mind.

Sounding overwhelmed, he brought up his aunt's upcoming eightieth birthday party.

"Did I mention it to you?" He asked.

"Not only did you "mention" it," I threw up air quotes, confused, "you asked if I'd be your plus one."

"Right, it's just I have a work meeting that day, and I have no idea when I'll even be arriving. I'm supposed to be the host. It's just a lot, and I don't know if it's a good idea that you attend anymore. I'll let you know."

This moment was in stark contrast to when he asked me to go with him. I didn't know what to think or how to feel. I was perplexed. Moreover, *I was hurt*.

His phone rang, and he answered, conducting a business call with a coworker for the amount of time it took for me to finish my wine. He was audibly agitated, and I was disguising my annoyance.

The shuttle ride to the stadium was rife with Nineteen's anxiety, and I felt it to my core. I tried being supportive and consoling, searching for positivity, but I was far from successful suggesting "let work go" for the night.

"Just be here with me." I encouraged.

It wasn't just his job that had him worked up, however. No pun intended.

During the fifteen-minute bus ride, he confided in me about family concerns that I had only secondhand experience in. His youngest nephew was struggling with a learning disability. I listened as the bus lurched right past Mr. Baby Crazy's condo downtown.*

I hoped that maybe once we got to the stadium, the overall mood would shift into a happier, more *pleasant* one. It did not.

"You're making things awkward." Nineteen accused me.

"I do it on purpose," I curtly replied, believing he was projecting.

---

*Of course, I noticed. I'd spent many a time on that sidewalk, parking my car or waiting for him to emerge from the garage doors. It was, after all, where he and I first met, and aside from Nineteen, he was the most significant relationship I'd partaken in during this entire online dating experience.

I sucked it all up from the moment we met at Union Station to when we left the stadium before the game ended. I felt so much anxiety I'd never felt around him before and I wasn't quite sure how to handle it yet.

This was my least gratifying date with Nineteen, and I didn't know what it meant. Even our goodnight kiss was disconnected. All I wanted was to hug him tighter, ease his mind, and *fix* whatever was bothering him, but he was doing everything to push me away, just short of actually physically shoving me. I drove home, my heart heavy, and desperately searching for that smile I wore so often after our dates. I wondered if I'd ever fully accept that I couldn't fix these kinds of things.

The time that passed between not seeing each other began making the times that we had spent together seem unreal. Had I imagined the magic? I guess this is what they mean by out of sight, out of mind. It was as if all the good that had been happening between us was a mere dream. He said we should see more of each other on date number two, so why was I seemingly being strung along now?

Sitting in Wednesday night therapy a week or so after our botched Dodger outing, I was talking about Nineteen and our conversation at brunch when I started laughing uncontrollably. The laughter, a coping mechanism, quickly dissolved into tears. I was feeling utterly lonely. Perhaps because some part of me knew that Nineteen wasn't ready to unpack with me after all. It was also August, which happens to be the month my mother died, so it's always a difficult time for me.

As I found myself writing the ending, I asked self-deprecating questions, like "Why don't I ever get a happy ending." I told myself things meant to console, like "Maybe this is just how your life is supposed to be" or "Maybe there's a silver lining somewhere." Part of the reason I believed I wasn't getting the happy ending was that I've always been so busy vigorously writing the ending before it's even allowed to begin. For thirty-three years, everything has ended and not happily ever after.

I attempted to put the metaphorical pen down, letting hope once again triumph over reason. Where did this endless amount of hope come from? Perhaps the answer to that is not as important as the answer to, "Why do I always want to write the ending before the plot has formed?"

In the week leading up to Nineteen's aunt's party, I went out and bought a very lovely, very expensive dress with shoes to match in the event that I would attend. It was a midi length, paisley number with short, ruched sleeves and a deep plunge neck. I decided I'd wear a modest black camisole underneath should Nineteen get his shit together and "let me know" that I was still his plus one.

Forty-eight hours before the event, he texted me:

It's best you not attend. I'm not even sure when I'll be arriving.

I wasn't planning on it.

I can come to the valley on Sunday to meet you for brunch.

Okay, sounds good. *thumbs up emoji*

What probably wasn't being conveyed was my deep disappointment. The problem with the thumbs-up emoji is that it's so passive-aggressive, and I'm often the only one who sees it as a big fuck you. Whatever needed to be said needed to be said face to face. When we met for brunch would be my opportunity to do so.

I returned the camisole to the store because when I did get the opportunity to wear that dress, it wouldn't be necessary to do so modestly. The day of the party was a sad one for me as I tried my best, without much success, to distract myself.

The following morning, I was en route to get a pedicure. Wondering how the party went and what time Nineteen was planning on coming over, I felt my phone buzz with a text message.

Morning. I'm sorry, I'm not going to make it for brunch. There is a mountain of things to do, not to mention clean up for the party. I can't leave my family to take care of it all. Plus, I still have to lesson plan for the week.

Was this guy for real? I contemplated using the middle finger emoji at that point. Who did he think he was? Better yet, who did he think *I* was?

I understand.

I was balancing on a tight wire somewhere between profound disappointment and my empathy for him. I was having a hard time understanding how we'd gotten here. After lying on his couch sharing music for hours, philosophical conversation, a handful of marathon dates, and chasing sunsets, this was not at all the direction I foresaw Nineteen and I going.

In the week following, I barely heard from him. He had yet to plan anything with me since canceling brunch. He finally reached out mid-week, asking if I wouldn't mind coming back to the South Bay that coming Friday night. I didn't mind.

It was a lovely mid-August evening, the coastal breeze relieving us of some of the thick of the summer heat. He emerged from his apartment building in a tight-fitting black tee, looking handsome as ever. We embraced, exchanging "Nice to see you's." We didn't have anything planned for this date, though I figured dinner was on the agenda once hunger inevitably struck.

"Would you mind hanging out with my brother for a bit and running an errand beforehand?"

Ugh, did he just punch me in the gut? Did this guy seriously want to drag me along on an errand before hanging out with his brother? It'd been almost two weeks since I'd seen him! Instead of replying with some passive-aggressive statement like I wanted to, I agreed with as much enthusiasm as I could feign. After all, I liked his brother, and I was looking forward to spending more time with him. I knew Nineteen and I would get time to ourselves at some point that evening.

The errand was Jo-Ann Fabrics at the Del Amo mall. His brother needed safety pins for some t-shirt hangtags. After grabbing agua frescas, we went on a hunt for the store. I didn't believe there was a Jo-Ann Fabrics inside the mall because he wasn't 100% sure where it was. I told him it was probably outside the mall in its own lot, and we playfully agreed to bet on it. No Google maps allowed. Whoever lost had to buy the first round of drinks wherever we ended up at the end of the night.

He won the bet. There was a Jo-Ann Fabrics in the mall. While perusing the stocked aisles of crafts and hobby-related paraphernalia, we joked and laughed with one another, reminding me of how just being in his presence brought joy. We didn't even need to be doing anything. I wondered if he felt the same way.

As we passed stocked rows of colorful yarn, I found out Nineteen used to knit. He took up a pastime as a distraction from destructive behavior (i.e., excessive drinking) in the aftermath of one of his called-off engagements. Envisioning the masculine, tatted-up Nineteen sitting in a rocking chair with a double point needle and bright ball of yarn in his lap while enjoying a glass of orange juice was no easy feat.

There was a flier for a knitting class at the checkout counter.

"I'm in need of a winter beanie." I teased, handing the flier to him. He and the clerk laughed.

En route to San Pedro to meet up with his brother, we listened to John Mayer's *Battle Studies* album while philosophizing about doing what we love versus doing what pays the bills.

"Sometimes, I just wanna run away from it all…some far off, foreign land, the hills of Spain…" He trailed off.

It was a mutual daydream of ours. I brought up the Miguel concert I had two tickets to in Santa Barbara that coming September. It was much closer than Spain and only a weekend getaway, but I still needed a plus one. I'd invited him once before without receiving the definitive "yes" I was looking for, and when *I* ask someone to be my plus one, I don't renege my invite. I didn't actually say that to him, but I was still feeling the sting of being invited to his aunt's eightieth and then not. We both needed a vacation and some quality time together.

He agreed, noticeably excited about the prospect of getting out of the city for the weekend. Maybe we were getting back on track here, I hoped. However, I still intended on broaching the topic of "us" once I snagged some alone time with him.

We joined his brother for Thai, dining al fresco. Nineteen brought up my trek from the valley for the third time since I arrived, thanking me for driving so far. He acted like he lived on the other side of the country.

"For the umpteenth time, it's *worth* it." I adamantly emphasized in front of our company, realizing he felt guilty about me often traveling almost forty miles in shitty LA traffic. If I couldn't convince him, maybe his next of kin could. I don't think he believed it, no matter how many times it was iterated. This broke my heart for him.

On more than one occasion during dinner, his brother snapped at him, making passive-aggressive comments about how Nineteen never had time for his own brother or anyone else. A couple of the digs were synonymous with my own thoughts and concerns. I got a strong sense that I wasn't the only one in his life feeling the lack of attention, and this said so much about how important he was to so many. This said so much about how much he was loved, and I could only hope he grasped that.

The strange part was how much I'd personally witnessed he'd do for his family, especially his brother, so why was his brother being so hard on him? This was surprising until I reminded myself that Nineteen lacked boundaries.

After dinner, we parted ways with his brother and decided to have drinks at The Bottle Inn, the quaint wine bar we stumbled upon during date number five.

"I feel like I'm being pushed away," I began as we sipped our wine at the end of the small bar, "Like things are suddenly disconnected between us."

He reacted as if he expected to have the conversation.

"It's completely understandable why you'd feel that way, and I planned on addressing this, myself, at some point tonight. You beat me to it."

He didn't deny it. He acknowledged that my feelings were valid. Defensiveness was nonexistent. *This was a good sign.*

In the midst of his explaining the distance that had become apparent over the past couple of weeks, I turned around to notice we were the last patrons. They were closing. We quickly finished our wine, and I paid since I'd lost the Jo-Ann Fabrics bet. We continued our discussion while walking the few blocks to the beach. It was a comfortable and breezy summer night.

"You may have noticed my brother has some animosity toward me, as well?" He asked.

"Yes, I noticed, but I wouldn't describe what I'm feeling as animosity."

I explained that I was concerned that if anything of quality was going to continue developing, we needed to see more of each other.

We had to maintain better communication if we sincerely wanted this to become what we claimed we were both looking for when we first met. I tried conveying the compassion and understanding I had for him when it came to his work and family, how I wanted to be supportive, but that I needed to feel like a priority in return.

Nineteen began explaining his burden in more depth and context, "When my dad is drunk and being an asshole to my mom, I'm the one she calls and complains to. I'm the youngest, but I'm the one without a family. I'm not married. I don't have kids, so I'm the go-to for everything."

He knew that having no boundaries wasn't good but felt obligated because of his single status and financial success. My heart broke over and over for him as I sat and listened to him open up.

"I understand, (*insert two-syllable name I came to adore*). I can't tell you how many times I watched my mother cry over my dad's addictive behavior. I once sat on a park bench with her in the middle of the day, rubbing her back, telling her it was going to be okay even though I had no idea if it was really going to be okay because I was *only seven years old*."

I am cautious with the words, "I understand." I believe they're often used as a means of consoling in uncomfortable situations when understanding is non-existent. But I honestly did understand.

Nineteen had become accustomed to this life so unconsciously in the past five years that even his therapist told him he was taking on too much. She said that his lifestyle was "unhealthy" and that he needed to "establish boundaries."

"I'm concerned that I'm incapable of giving you or us what's deserved." He confessed.

"I don't know about you, but I've been on a lot of dates, and none of them have felt remotely close to or similar to what you and I share. It's not every day we come across someone we feel this type of connection with. But, it's worth trying." I countered.

He looked at me, torn.

"I agree," he nodded, turning his head to stare into the blackness, the only certainty that we were at water's edge being the sound of the Pacific lapping onto the shore. The nearby lamppost shone just enough light on Nineteen's profile for me to see the angst and the sadness.

"How do you feel about me making my way to the South Bay once or twice during the week and every weekend?"

"I can't ask you to do that."

"What if you don't have to ask me? What if I tell you I'm just going to do it?" After some hesitation, this seemed to work for him.

I'd never felt closer to him than before that night. This was proof that connection stretches far beyond the physical realm. We were two human beings, communicating their fears and desires for the salvation of something we both deemed worth fighting for. I knew it was unfortunate we had to fight that early on, but something in me kept telling me it was worth it. *He was worth it*. We both deserved happiness, and for the most part, we'd been making each other very happy.

When we got back to his place, we lay on his bed staring up at the ceiling in the low, warm light, listening to John Mayer's *Battle Studies* album from front to back for the second time that night. Somewhere in between the "Edge of Desire" and "Friends, Lovers, or Nothing," I straddled him on the bed. Our eyes locked as my hair hung down in a brunette halo around our heads. The thick strands cast soft shadows across his pensive face.

"Write a verse about this moment…right here…right now." He insisted, my face hovering close enough to feel the air escape his mouth.

I was so distracted by the beauty of his unexpected request, the words I ended up giving him weren't spectacular, in my opinion, though he liked them. We kissed and then we made love.

In the week that passed after Nineteen let me in ever so slightly, driving to the South Bay during a school night proved difficult for me due to some work deadlines. I made plans to meet him Friday night after work at the Del Amo mall. We were going to see the new Winnie the Pooh movie, *Christopher Robin*, after grabbing dinner.

We agreed to meet at Frida's, a Mexican restaurant. He was running slightly late, so I sat at the bar enjoying a glass of sangria before his arrival. I was nervous waiting for him. Even though we'd been dating for a bit at that point, he always gave me the good jitters.

Sneaking up behind me when he arrived, we embraced as he grazed my cheek with a kiss. There was quite a bit of time to kill before the movie, so we conversed over a couple more glasses of sangria at the bar.

"I'll take sweatpants or casual attire over a fancy dress-up outfit every time," he complimented my casual plaid shirt over a red camisole and jeans.

"Thank you," I flushed under his gaze.

After drinks, we walked through the mall to pass the time. I was in the market for a couch, and Nineteen was looking for a birthday gift for his sister. He wrapped his arm around my shoulder while we walked, and I appreciated the affection, returning it with my arm around his waist. This was the first time he'd been publicly affectionate with me since our parking meter kiss. Walking around a furniture store gave me a glimpse into what it might be like if we kept doing this dating thing well into the future. I liked the feeling it gave me and the imagery it conjured up. It was a feeling of home, perhaps of family.

We stopped in Anthropologie, where he asked my opinion on gift choices for his sister whose birthday was coming up. I liked the feeling his inclusion gave me and hoped all of these feelings were mutual.

After shopping, we got sushi for dinner when he confessed, "It's refreshing to have conversations with depth. As I've said before, you're the first person I've gone past one date with in five years, and I'm really enjoying your company."

Apparently, he'd found himself on many a date with super shallow women, the kind of shallow whose favorite musician is Jennifer Lopez and her only passion is makeup. I dropped my chopsticks at the thought of someone's favorite musician being Jennifer Lopez.*

After two failed engagements, a shallow woman was safe, I thought. She'd never be too close for comfort.

As we shared laughs over some unfiltered sake and tasty spicy tuna, he told me he'd written a verse, as well, the night he asked me to write one as I straddled his body in the soft glow of the bedside lamp. I was surprised to hear this, acknowledging how unsatisfied I was with my impromptu writing.

"It was good. I liked it!" he said.

"Give me some time to come up with something better before you share yours."

"Okay, sure." He smiled.

---

*Don't get me wrong – she's a lot of things, a fabulous dancer and total babe, namely, but she is *not* a musician.

I adore that smile, I thought.

After dinner, we still had more time to kill before the movie. It was getting chilly, so we stepped inside an Old Navy so he could buy a sweater. As we stood in the very long line, my impatience got the best of me. Patience has never been my forte.

"Okay, I can't wait. Tell me what you wrote, please!"

With that grin I'd grown to love, he pulled out his phone and opened the memos application. He handed me his phone without saying a word, and this is what I read:

From the Bottle Inn

To being lost in your hair

Discovering a new stare

Within this moment's whim

I lost my breath for half a second underneath the bright, fluorescent lights of an American retail chain. I felt like he'd just reached inside my chest, squeezed my heart, and rearranged all of the atoms and cells that make me who I am.

This was no longer just dating. This was no longer just a book about twenty different online dates. I was falling in love. After I read his words, I felt like the feeling was mutual. I wanted to throw my arms around him, profess my love for him the way Jessie Ware commanded in her song, "Say You Love Me."

Instead, I said, "Text that to me, please," with as much calmness as I could muster while handing him his phone back.

I didn't want to unveil the love my heart had just exploded with. I feared scaring him away while he was vulnerable. It's the unexpected moments like that that keep the endless hope burning alive and well inside of me, the seemingly minute exchanges that project more volume than a live rock concert.

The movie, *Christopher Robin*, was wonderful. It was a late showing, and at one point, I got so sleepy, I rested my head on Nineteen's shoulder. He returned the gesture by resting his head on mine. For a moment, time stood still while Mr. Robin rediscovered the joys of life alongside his furry, red shirt-clad companion, and I rediscovered love.

EVEN AS THE RED FLAG FLEW

Too much time passed between communicating, and there was nothing planned for the following weekend. I didn't hear from Nineteen for almost an entire week after our movie outing. Everything that had culminated between us was crumbling into a massive black hole of "did that really happen?" Was I giving someone the *Benefit of the Doubt* when he didn't deserve it?

The only thing that seemed to help was to stay busy, and staying busy consisted of going to a bar in Sherman Oaks with my friend and giving my number to an incredibly inebriated man who didn't speak English. Of course, I had no intention of ever answering his advances, but the very act of flirting made me feel better, temporarily. I didn't want any of that. *I wanted Nineteen*.

I tried calling Nineteen the next day, with the intent of telling him exactly how I felt. Our weekend getaway to Santa Barbara was fast approaching. If there's one thing I can't stand, it's when people make such commitments and back out at the last moment. Nineteen had already exhibited a propensity for such behavior.

I'd had these concert tickets for months, and I wasn't about to end up solo at a Miguel concert. When I'd initially purchased the tickets, I was single, not even dating, but I adored Miguel. A man who wrote a song titled “The Pussy is Mine” is not solo-concert-going material. He’s sexy with a lover concert-going material. I bought two tickets in the hopes I was manifesting something. Nineteen confessed that he, too, had purchased two tickets to Coachella for two years straight, with the intent of bringing a significant other. He always wound up taking a friend. I was *not* taking a friend to a Miguel concert.

He finally returned my call about an hour after I reached out to him, which gave me time to consume a bit of liquid courage. He informed me that he was busy celebrating a family member’s birthday the entire weekend.

“You can call me back if I’m interrupting something,” he said.

“No, I answered the phone because I make time for the things and people I want to make time for.”

My brusque statement landed its intended impact, and he acknowledged that he hadn’t been doing a very good job of making time for us, instantly apologetic. I reiterated how difficult it was for me to continue putting forth an effort when he didn't meet me at least forty percent of the way, if not half.

“I want to do a better job at meeting you halfway. I know this hasn’t been fair and I’m still committed to Santa Barbara.”

We made plans for him to come to my place the following Saturday. The week leading up to our date night, he maintained better communication, and I was hopeful once again.

John Mayer's lyrics from his song, "Edge of Desire," about willingly going back on the things he believes played on repeat in my mind. I wondered if I was going back on the things I believed?

When Saturday rolled around, I received a text message from Nineteen while running errands.

I'm going to have to cancel. I'm probably going to be at work late.

I told him I wasn't going to accept his cancellation - that he could be late and we could do absolutely nothing, but that he wasn't going to cancel on me. *Not this time*. He accepted my non-acceptance.

He showed up around 6 p.m. I'd made an impromptu salmon dinner for us, the first time I ever cooked for him. We sat at my dining table discussing politics and other not-so-light fares. Post-meal, we watched videos exchanged in his family group chat of his youngest nephew's potty training. Of course, anything involving a toilet was out of bounds during courtship, so while I found it sweet that he wanted to share this with me, the lack of boundaries was deafening!

While he engaged in the family group conversation, I wondered why this couldn't wait until later? I always liked the idea of being close to family, especially since I didn't have anything remotely close to that. But just how close is close enough?

I offered him the option of going out, but he preferred to stay in. It had been almost two weeks since we'd seen each other, so I was content with lying on my living room floor listening to music when I was able to pry him away from the group chat. We listened to the entire Harry Styles album front to back because Nineteen swore it was "unexpectedly wonderful." And it was. Maybe it wasn't so much the music that was wonderful, but the fact that Nineteen was lying on my living room floor next to me, our skin occasionally grazing one another. We could have been listening to Barney, the Purple Dinosaur theme song for all I care. As always, I loved our tendency to do everything with music, to be able to lie there and listen to an entire album together.

We began making out, to which I quipped, "I do have a bed, ya know" He chuckled and stood up, holding out his hand, leading me to my bedroom.

We had sex, and I gave him head for the first time. Afterward, we watched some of KCRW's tiny desk concerts. Somewhere between being introduced to the amazing musician/artist Tash Sultana and delighting in the evening's postcoital pleasures, Nineteen insinuated that he couldn't stay.

"*You're leaving*?"

"Yeah, is that okay?" He heard my shock, "I have an early day tomorrow and have to ready my lesson plans for the week."

I told him it was okay, but it wasn't. There was nothing okay about the fact that he was going to leave around midnight after having just fucked me, after having not seen me for a long time, after I just had his dick in my mouth for the first time! Even as the red flag flew, I rationalized his actions for the good of my fragile heart, for the undying hope within me that maybe, just maybe, I chose wisely this time. *I went back on the things I believed.*

JUNOT DIAZ SAID, THIS IS HOW YOU LOSE HER

He showed up at my place an hour late the following Friday morning for our weekend getaway to Santa Barbara. We had plans to attend the concert at the Santa Barbara Bowl that evening, among a few other activities, including a tasting tour of Santa Ynez's Bridlewood Winery on Sunday morning.

While driving northbound on the 101, he took a couple of work-related phone calls before relaying that his brother had tried to have an intervention with him a few days prior. His brother was concerned that Nineteen was "married to his work," and he was trying to stop it before it was "too late." I asked him how that went while silently agreeing with his brother.

"Not well," he replied with resentment in his voice and a frown I'd met the night he shared his obligations as the unattached child in his family.

I figured that wouldn't sit well with him. If his brother couldn't get through to him about his dual stress-inducing careers, then I might as well keep my opinions to myself. I also thought he should be having an intervention with his entire family. I believe they call that establishing healthy boundaries.

During the drive, he was noticeably distant. There wasn't much physical contact at all and zero affection. During our first stop, Sunstone Winery in Santa Ynez (the same one where Mr. Baby Crazy told me I could take five months off of work to care for our firstborn), I asked Nineteen if he was all right. Apparently, I'd asked it one too many times. He was agitated with my question, defensively claiming he was "fine." I tried to check my empathy at the grapevine, but I couldn't. I felt his energy, and it was averse to everything that was happening, everything he was claiming.

We were in beautiful wine country during the first weekend of fall, the season we both proclaimed to be our favorite. The sun was setting, and the crisp, cool air was tangible. I wanted nothing more than to shower this man with the residual fragments of my explosive lyric-reading heart. I knew, however, that was not the proper course of action. I knew my idea to have a romantic weekend getaway should have been chucked out the window somewhere along the coast between his resentment toward his brother and his phone calls with coworkers.

"I used to be just like you, Lindsay; heart on the sleeve, endlessly hopeful." A bottle of wine in, he began opening up about just how "fine" he was. "At some point, I built these walls, and I'm afraid they're indestructible. I didn't even realize how strong they were until I was with you."

I wanted to believe Nineteen was worth fighting for, that *we* were worth fighting for, but every time I met his wall, a part of that belief tarnished. My instincts knew that when Nineteen feared his walls were indestructible, they probably were. It was relieving to hear the truth from him, though, to listen to the self-awareness he so willingly exhibited. As I stated before, I'd rather hear the truth than what someone thinks I want to hear, and at least his honesty meant I didn't imagine things.

We made our way back to the Airbnb to get ready for the concert. We were staying in an adorable basement turned two-bed, one-bath living space of a home situated atop a cliff, overlooking the Pacific Ocean in Summerland, California. You could see it from the 101 freeway, just a short drive south of Santa Barbara. An empty koi pond directly to the left of the entrance mirrored Nineteen's mood.

We didn't have much time before the concert, so I got ready quickly. My attire consisted of a sexy velour top with a lariat necklace that rested between my noticeable cleavage, no bra, and a burnout velour wrap dress worn as a kimono over denim high-waisted jeans. Surely, this ensemble would garner some attention, if only sexual, from Nineteen, I thought. Nada. Nothing. *Zilch*. I don't even recall receiving a "you look nice."

***Bonus Pro Dating Tip:* Always compliment your date's appearance.**

That's okay, I told myself. I felt sexy, and I was ready for a sexy concert performed by one of the sexiest artists in the business at one of my favorite venues. If my sexy outfit couldn't conjure up some sexual energy in my lackluster date, surely Miguel could!

It was a beautiful night, and Miguel played most of my favorite songs. At one point, Nineteen reached over and placed his right hand on my thigh, though not keeping it there for long. I could feel how difficult this action was for him, almost forced. I was heartbroken. He couldn't allow himself joy, for God's sake! Not to mention, I had to work hard, emotionally, to remind myself that his lack of presence had nothing to do with me. I reached over, showing my affection on more than one occasion, thankfully never rejected.

Arriving back at our accommodations, we showered and got comfortable. We sat across from one another in the living room and listened to music while talking. Nineteen barely moved during the concert, though, claimed he "really enjoyed it." On the other hand, I danced consistently and sang along to most of the songs. It appeared Miguel's repetitive chanting, "I wanna fuck tonight," didn't elicit much of a response from Nineteen, though that's precisely what we did before going to sleep.

We walked to Red Kettle Coffee from our Airbnb the following morning, followed by a brief stroll down Summerland's main drag. The sky was grey and the air cool but comfortable as we dined outdoors at a breakfast café. I wanted to make him French toast at the Airbnb, but he'd killed that plan when he randomly mentioned that he didn't like "sweets" for breakfast. The man with the self-proclaimed sweet tooth said this in casual conversation before knowing my plan to make us breakfast in bed. When I relayed this to him, he felt bad, but we laughed about it. At the café, he saw a waiter bring out a plate of French toast.

"Mmm, that looks good," Nineteen's eyes followed the plate to a nearby table.

"If you order the French toast, I'll never forgive you."

"I wouldn't do that," he chuckled.

The waiter approached our table, and Nineteen asked him what he recommended.

"The French Toast is really popular."

We giggled before I gave him the evil eye that said, "don't you dare."

During breakfast, he suggested visiting a couple of Santa Barbara museums. We spent the afternoon exploring the Museum of Contemporary Art and one other museum before finding our way to East Beach and plopping ourselves down in the sand. Under the September sun, Nineteen and I killed a bottle of wine he'd been carrying around in the trunk of his car while partaking in one of our favorite pastimes - people watching.

The uncomfortably cold ocean wind whipped at my bare skin as we observed a group of adults playing a game neither of us had ever seen before. I laid my head on his shoulder in between comments about passersby and burrowed my body next to his. This was primarily to shield me from the biting wind but also to show my affection. Even if I was expecting a response, I knew I wasn't going to get one. The lack of physical contact made me think of our epic first date when we sat outside on a park bench, people watching. If people were watching us now, they'd presume we'd been together for a while, and that we may be in need of reigniting something.

After the beach, we drove our windblown, sun-kissed selves near the downtown Santa Barbara restaurant I'd made reservations. Then, we strolled into an empty sports bar where we sat down at the bar to order a drink.

"Wanna play pool?" We asked each other at the same time. We smiled.

"That was crazy," I laughed.

"It's not really that unusual. We both saw the pool tables at the same time."

This response was a far cry from the guy who once texted me "like minds who think about each other" after we bid each other a good night text at the same time.

It was the first time we'd ever played pool together, and I almost won. I wish I had.

We ate dinner at Black Sheep, a fusion restaurant. The food was spectacular, and the conversation was surprisingly as remarkable. We conversed about race and identity over Peruvian potato tacos and scallop crudo before I told him the synopsis of the book I was writing. He knew I was writing but didn't know what it was about until that moment. I even told him that he was Nineteen in the whole twenty-dates challenge, deliberately leaving out the part where I hoped I didn't make it to twenty. He didn't seem the least bit bothered by the subject of my book, which was relieving. In fact, he offered up some of his perspectives toward online dating and the progress I was making.

"All online dating is a digital handshake," he stated, and he was right. It isn't much different than meeting someone in person. The pros lay in that one could potentially weed out the not-so-great within a short five minutes or less.

"Have you given yourself a deadline for the rough draft?"

"Well, no, but I suppose I should?"

He gave me welcomed advice. "Give yourself a solid deadline to work toward, or the procrastination will prevail."

This was the most relaxed I'd felt all weekend. It probably had to do with all of the alcohol I'd consumed but anything to ease the stresses his unpredictable behavior was causing.

After dinner, we decided to head back to the Airbnb and "chill" for the rest of the night. There was wine there, and we were beat after gallivanting around town all day, spending extended time in the sun. Plus, we had to get up early for the tour I'd reserved at the Santa Ynez winery.

He walked to the nearby liquor store for bottled water while I showered. When he returned, he began taking photos of the unique features of the interior with his professional camera. It was one of the things I admired most about Nineteen. He was incredibly intelligent, the kind of analytical intelligence that could successfully build an electric bike all by himself while simultaneously teaching you how to develop and code a website. Yet, he still had so many creative hobbies. His mind was the best of both worlds. All of the times I'd been allowed in were extraordinary. It was a beautiful place full of depths I looked forward to spending more time in, a place I'd been falling in love with, quite possibly, since our first visit to The Bottle Inn.

After taking photos, he showered and joined me in the living room in our respective spots from the night before. By this time, it was around eleven 'o'clock in the evening. We were taking turns sharing songs while his phone intermittently buzzed with text messages from family members and coworkers. He responded while I sat there, across from him, with my bare legs propped up on the chair in front of me. The alcohol I'd consumed during the day was catching up to me, and my head was a little fuzzy. I was trying not to overreact about the fact that most of his attention was being directed toward his phone, toward the place where we'd first had our digital handshake.

"Am I boring you?" I blurted out.

Inquiring minds just wanted to fucking know.

He sharply inhaled, slowly turning his phone around to show me that he was searching for the next song to play on YouTube. We both knew that it was about more than that, however. He took another deep breath in before uttering five words that knocked the wind out of me.

"I can't do this anymore."

I frantically searched for my breath or a rewind button, feeling like a cat whose claws failed her after leaping. I was dizzy, my mind reeling from his unexpected declaration. *What the fuck did that mean? Oh my God, I think he's ending this.*

I had a hard time fathoming how quickly my head could go from resting easy in Nineteen's lap while sharing our love for folk music and John Mayer to him telling me he couldn't do this, do *us*, anymore. How did we arrive there after sitting across from each other enjoying a wonderful meal over the equally wonderful conversation? None of this made sense. How did we get here? How did this happen? I would later ask myself all these questions repeatedly.

"I can't keep dragging you along like this. I told myself I'm going to go away with Lindsay, and I'm not going to think about work or any other responsibilities, and I haven't even been able to do that," he stated.

That's undoubtedly true, I thought. *Okay, so he's not oblivious. There's still hope. Fucking hope*. I cursed hope while simultaneously searching for the fix-it tools.

I excused myself to the bathroom to throw cold water on my face. I stared at my makeup-less, inebriated face in the mirror, and I think I was asking someone, something, God maybe, what to do. Shoving back the tears, I took a deep breath before returning to the living room. He was sitting in the rocking chair, sullen.

"I'm not letting you do this. This isn't a decision you make alone."

"This isn't up to you," he scoffed, "Lindsay, you deserve more than I can give you."

Oh, the irony! My whole life, I've been questioning if I'm ever enough, and I fall for someone who seemingly doesn't think he's enough for me. I felt my eyes welling up with hot tears. I suppose my hope in wanting to have a say in the final decision lay in wanting Nineteen to realize that my faith was stronger than his guilt.

Was this premeditated, I briefly wondered. No, surely no one plans on ending a relationship when you're a hundred miles from home during what is supposed to be a romantic weekend. *Or do they*?

"I know you've been feeling the rejection. It's not fair to you, and I can't keep being reminded of my failings. It's a selfish decision, but one that I have to make."

He then rattled off all of his obligations from his two full-time jobs to being there for his family.

While trying to make sense of the selfish part, I stood up and walked over to him. Bending over, I cradled his face in my hands and attempted to kiss him. He turned his face in pain. The rejection was nauseating, almost bringing me to my knees.

"Please kiss me."

"*We're talking, Lindsay*."

"I know, and we're not done talking. Please *just kiss me*."

He managed to return a meager kiss. It was my way of showing him that I wasn't giving up. I returned to my seat.

My heart was somewhere beneath my feet scattered about the wooden floor, begging for Kintsugi – anything to remedy the unexpected destruction. *Put the pieces back together, Nineteen. It's imperfect, but it's beautiful*. I cried inside.

"So, you're telling me that you're so overwhelmed with life and its responsibilities that you have to give something up in your busy schedule, and the thing you're choosing to give up is the *one* thing that actually makes *you* happy?" I asked him.

"Yes," he answered without hesitation.

In the silence, I choked back tears.

"You're making a big mistake."

"Maybe."

In the short three months that we'd been getting to know each other, I recognized the stubbornness in him because I was just as, if not more, stubborn. He was as adamant as I was about many things, and it wasn't surprising that he wasn't going to change his mind even if he thought he was *maybe* making a mistake.

"Then just tell me that this isn't what you want, that this is something you feel like you have to do. I need to hear that truth from you, at least."

"I don't want this," he confirmed, again without hesitation.

Whether he didn't want to be ending us or just told me what he thought I needed to hear is not as important as the fact that I believed him. This made me feel minutely better while also releasing the reservoir of grief. In some small way, it gave me more hope than I already had that this wasn't *it*. *This wasn't over*. He'd come around. He just needed some time.

Turning my back on him, I allowed the waterworks to flow. What was I trying to hide? This was fucking sad, and his eyes were watery, too.

I spun around back toward him, this time a slight tinge of venom in my voice, "This isn't on me. I'm not the one writing the end of this story. *This is on you*. I'm not the one walking away."

I paused.

Continuing, I told him, "Everybody Leaves" was going to be the tentative title of my first book (the one you're reading now).

"That's a great title," he replied.

"It's a horrible title," I countered, knowing we were both talking about two separate things. Nineteen was talking about the title of a book, and I was talking about the hard truth, and here he was, *leaving me, leaving us*.

I finally had the answer to the question he asked me on our second date: "How could I fuck this up?" *This. This is how you fuck it up*. If he'd fucked it up on the second date over Dodger dogs and friendly banter, it wouldn't be as hard as it was now. At least the drive to spatial separation wouldn't have been hours long. The drive could have been non-existent. Hell, I could have Ubered! I was devastated. I couldn't believe I was stuck in Summerland with no way home but Nineteen and his stupid Mustang.

"I've never met anyone who sees me the way you do. I believe I see you, too. I want you to know I'm grateful for the time we've spent together, and I'll always be grateful for having met you."

"I'm grateful for all of it, too," he agreed.

Isn't all of this enough to not want to quit? I wondered in anguish. The walls that Nineteen described were as indestructible as he claimed, no matter how Big, Bad Wolf I wanted to huff and puff them down.

I'd texted a good friend back in LA almost as soon as the disparaging words, "I can't do this anymore," were uttered. She was on a weekend getaway of her own with her best friend near the Palm Springs desert. Upon receiving my unexpected message, she was ready to drive the three and a half hours to pick me up. I told her I'd be fine, that I just needed some sleep, but I was thankful that I was no longer alone in the knowledge of this ending, this *nonsense*.

I crawled into bed shortly after our conversation ended. Nineteen began getting ready for bed.

"I'm gonna sleep on the couch."

"We still care about each other, right?" I protested, "You are not sleeping on the couch. Sleep in this bed with me, *please*."

He agreed. We embraced after he crawled underneath the covers. I asked him to kiss me before we fell asleep. I don't know if I was feeling for more answers, in the dark, somewhere between his lips, on the surface of his tongue, or in his arms. I didn't find any answers. I just knew that I needed that last physical comfort from him if this was going to be the last time I ever lay next to him. He kissed me, and somehow, I quickly fell asleep.

INNER BATTLE STUDIES

The morning I woke up in Summerland next to a man who was the closest thing I'd ever come to what I wanted was one of those mornings I woke up rudely reminded of the ending that had transpired the night before. I woke up before Nineteen, gathering my thoughts through the fog of heavy slumber, wishing it was all a bad dream.

I crept out of bed into the kitchen, where my phone was left charging overnight. I needed to get a hold of Bridlewood winery to cancel the tour, or they'd charge me for a no-show. So I went into the spare bedroom, the furthest room away from where Nineteen was still sleeping and the room where we'd had sex for what was unknowingly the last time.

I had a couple of text messages from my friend I'd reached out to the night before. It was a slew of what happened's, what-the-fucks, and are-you-okays concluding with:

He's a fucking asshole.

It was the latter I had the most difficult time processing. Nineteen wasn't an asshole. He was far from it, so how could he do this and this weekend of all times? Not that there's ever an opportune moment to break up with someone. I can see why people that cared about me would deem him an asshole. I found myself wishing we weren't in Santa Barbara and contemplating calling a very expensive Uber.

The answers to any of my friend's questions were too long to respond to. I wasn't even entirely sure I had any answers, so I searched for the number to Bridlewood. The winery, however, didn't even open until 11 a.m., the time of our reservation. So, I had no choice but to call the credit card company I'd made the reservation in and claim I'd misplaced my card. I felt like such an asshole, an asshole for lying about losing my card, and an asshole for the fact that this winery was going to experience a no-show. It was completely against my morals, but then again, breaking up with someone on a weekend getaway is too. At least I hadn't been the asshole to commit that asshole act. Great, Nineteen and I were both making asshole moves this weekend. *See?* We were perfect for one another!

I assuaged my guilt with the thought that while the staff at Bridlewood and Capital One might not sympathize with what was actually happening, I'm sure they've all experienced a breakup once or thrice before. I was doing what I had to do when Nineteen woke up and emerged from the bedroom.

We exchanged some awkward hey's as he made a beeline to the bathroom for a shower. I began packing and cleaning up the place. It was early, barely 9:30, when Nineteen retreated to the patio. He was lounging in one of the chairs, enjoying the Sunday morning ocean air underneath a cloudless, cerulean blue sky, when I walked outside and sat down next to him. We exchanged some small talk pleasantries (something we mutually claimed profound disdain for) about how nice the weather was before the silence took over. It didn't take me long to go back inside, taking extra special note of the empty koi pond. While in Japan, I recalled reading that Koi fish symbolized good luck, fortune, and perseverance in adversity.

I went to the kitchen sink to see him through the window without his knowledge. Studying his sun-drenched profile, his strong jawline, and the coarse facial hair that often left me with a welcomed blemish or two after a make-out session, I took it all in. It felt like a moment not many have the luxury of having: If tomorrow were your last day, what would you do with the remaining time? Only this was like if this is the last moment you get to look at him, like *really look at him*, what will you do with that moment? How will you take it all in? I felt it a strange sort of privilege.

What I saw at that moment was nothing outwardly. I saw the sadness, the burdening pensiveness, and the heaviness protruding from Nineteen like a neon-colored cloud. I could still see this man as part of my future while knowing it was over. This was the last time I'd get to study that profile, that mole under his beautiful, brown eye, his wavy brown hair, and all of the internal intricacies that seeped through the walls of his deeply insulated fort. It's one of the oddest feelings to date to see something so clearly but be conscious that what I was seeing and what I was feeling was not what was going to be.

Shortly after leaving him alone, he came inside and sat down at the dining table across from me.

"Were you able to cancel the winery tour?"

"No," I deliberately left out all of the other shitty details about how I canceled my credit card.

"Would it be weird if we still went?" he asked, met with my surprised expression. And even though it was fucking weird, I told him that it wasn't.

"We're both adults who enjoy each other's company, so I believe we can handle a winery tour." I professed.

"It's a beautiful day. We shouldn't waste it," He added incentive.

I nodded in agreement. Maybe this was *his* way of looking at me through the kitchen window.

We would have been on time for the tour if it weren't for the speeding ticket Nineteen received three minutes away from the winery. The police officer was one of the nicest I've ever encountered. As he and Nineteen chatted about the lack of technology used in giving tickets, I couldn't help but think that this was some level of mercy having karma. That karma said, "*Hey Nineteen, here's a really expensive speeding ticket for breaking up with that amazing woman in your passenger seat when you really don't want to during what was supposed to be a romantic weekend getaway, but, hey*

Nineteen, forget about me and go enjoy the winery," which is exactly what the cop said to him before we drove off.

"Forget about me and go enjoy the winery."

I may not have won the pool game the night before, but the thought of him receiving that upwards of $500 ticket in the mail delivered a tinge of solace.

Two couples and the tour guide were impatiently awaiting our arrival. The tour began in the vineyard. Nineteen and I hadn't eaten anything for breakfast, so we quickly felt the alcohol. Our guide snapped photos of the couples in front of a picturesque backdrop; acres of lovely rolling hills covered in neatly planted aisles of grapevines splashed in bright, afternoon sunlight against a saturated blue sky. I purposely stood off to the side, a bit disconnected from the group and Nineteen, hoping that the guide wouldn't offer to take our photo. Of course, he offered.

"Sure!" Nineteen enthusiastically obliged, handing the tour guide his phone.

I don't have a poker face, so I wonder if anyone saw my eyes roll or the pain this staged photo was causing me. I posed next to him with a smile, though, not with my arm around him. He had his arm slightly around my back, clad in his stupid Kelly Kapowski from *Saved by the Bell* white sleep shirt. It was the cleanest thing he'd packed that wouldn't have him sweating under the high noon Santa Ynez sun.

The whole thirty seconds were awkward, only serving as an additional punch to my dilapidated gut. I felt like a phony, wondering what these nice people would think if they knew he'd just broken up with me twelve hours ago.

We went inside for the tasting, where each of us blindly tasted wine from a black glass. We had to guess the varietal, the year, and the cost. This turned out to be a lot more fun than I'd anticipated, and for the span of half an hour, I almost forgot that our relationship was over. When my wine-induced brain awakened to reality, my heart began to ache at the thought that this was some of the last fun we were ever going to have together.

I went to pay for the tour and asked for a bottle of some of the delicious zinfandel we'd tried during the tasting. I'd never tasted zinfandel I liked as much as Bridlewood's.

"The zin is only available to members." The tour guide attempted to sell Nineteen and I a single winery membership reasonably under the impression that we were a *couple*.

Nineteen and I exchanged a buzzed glance before he encouraged me to join.

"It'll be a good excuse to return and do some of your writing! You said, yourself, you want to come up here more frequently."

He was right.

As innocent as his reminder was, it served as an insult to injury. When I said I wanted to go there more frequently, I'd hoped it wouldn't be alone.

I deliberated for a very short period.

"What the hell!" I threw up my hands.

I bought a branded wine opener Nineteen was eyeing. I grabbed the beautifully etched piece out of his hand and placed it on the counter, prompting an "Are you sure" from him. Of course, I was sure.

We decided to immediately take advantage of my member's benefits and explore the "member's only" grounds. Alongside the dirt trail and a beautiful babbling brook were two former racehorses and several weeping willows, one of my favorite tree species. I felt reality settling in again. This would be our last walk together.

Interrupting the hollow sound of our feet on the gravel trail, I said, "I'm having such a wonderful time, and I'm having a difficult time believing this is over. This just doesn't make any sense to me."

There was an awkward silence.

"I understand." He eventually replied.

His trite response didn't comfort me. He didn't understand.

It was nearing 3 p.m. after we grabbed a bite to eat and decided to head home. I felt like my emotions had just gone twelve rounds in the ring with Manny Pacquiao.

Nineteen fittingly chose John Mayer's *Battle Studies* album as the soundtrack, and for forty-six minutes and thirty-six seconds, it stung like a thousand hornets, disturbed from their nest. Aside from John Mayer's melodic voice and poignant lyrics, it was a mostly silent, almost three-hour, ending.

Summerland passed as I craned my neck, peering over the freeway into the green, verdant hills dotted with colorful coastal structures.

"Can you see it?" He asked knowingly.

Could I see the Airbnb behind the emerald green roof we just spent two nights in? Or could I see the place where he voluntarily gave up on this, gave up on *us*? What was he asking if I could see?

An hour later, I broke the unbearable silence again, between stifling tears, "A part of me understands your decision, but a part of me still doesn't…and I'm horrible at goodbyes. *I hate them*. I can't say goodbye to you when we get to my place."

"I've been having an inner battle with myself, as well," he admitted.

I waited, hoping he'd elaborate on his statement, but there was nothing.

I turned my head to stare out the window at the green hills so he wouldn't see the tears finally spilling over somewhere around the city of Camarillo.

These were the last moments I was going to spend in the presence of a person who made me feel better than anyone before him. Aside from commitment-phobic Mr. East Coast, Nineteen had shown me the closest glimpse of all I've ever wanted, of all I've been searching for.

Pulling up to my apartment a little over an hour later after his inner battle statement, he helped me carry my things upstairs. All I could hear was the sound of our footsteps and my accelerated heartbeat. Dreading the moment of goodbye in my living room, I turned to face him, taking a deep audible breath as my eyes reluctantly met his.

He took a deep breath, himself, before breaking the perpetual silence, "I'm not saying I just want to disappear from your life. I just need to figure some things out...Like you said, we do have a connection and...I think we should still talk."

I responded with an embrace that lasted longer than any we'd ever given each other. I didn't say goodbye. I didn't say anything at all. I didn't think it would be the last time I saw him walk away. I locked the door behind him then keeled over into a ball on the hardwood floor. I was finally and fully able to liberate the tears. An hour later, he texted me the photos he took of us during the weekend. I responded with the photos I'd taken but again, no words and no goodbye from either one of us.

EAST OF EDEN

Ellen, a dear, longtime friend, showed up at my apartment when I returned home from Santa Barbara. She put her domestic duties on hold and watched me drink my sorrows to the bottom of a wine bottle, and I'm ever so grateful. Of course, I'll never forget what she said to me, either.

With rancor in her voice, "I'm so tired of these men using you to teach themselves valuable lessons in life."

It wasn't the first time she'd seen me get my heart broken by a man. Hell, it was the second time that year alone, and I knew what she meant. Though I appreciated her concern, I also began to see the situation differently. Maybe I needed to see it from a different perspective to spare me some heartache. Regardless, I began expressing gratitude for playing that part in these men's lives, if that was, in fact, the part I was playing. It wasn't like I was coming away with nothing. I, too, was learning valuable lessons.

My best friend, Norma, also showed up at my door that night. She stopped to give me a hug, a hug I didn't even know I needed as much as that one. After both she and Ellen left, I needed some fresh air. I walked out into the night, hair still wet from the shower I hoped would wash away my grief, the late September breeze sending a chill up my spine. I kept walking, guided by an almost full moon. It was under that light I began feeling the profundity of what I'd lost. I'll be the first to exclaim how much grey area there is in life, but sometimes, we need only look at the black and white of a situation. At that moment, the black and white was that two people were alone again, two amazing people who had the kind of connection that doesn't come around often. It was the kind of connection that when you feel it, something in your gut, heart, mind, your very soul grabs hold and never allows you to forget it. The black and white was walking underneath the moonlight on a beautiful fall evening, *alone*.

Less than forty-eight hours later, the anger found me. Alas, this is the cycle of grief. I saw the visual that usually comes to mind when anger overwhelms my psyche: my fist driving itself through drywall or a hollow door. The anger lay in that he *left*. He *left* after he said he wasn't that person. He *left* after everything we meant to each other. He *left* after so many had left him. He *left* just like everyone else because *Everybody. Fucking. Leaves.*

Grief is an ugly cycle. I'm not sure what I do to stop it or to postpone it, at least, but I know keeping busy is key. Distraction always helps…and wine. There's always wine. But anyone who has ever used alcohol as a means of coping knows that it eventually shoves all our careful packing into neatly semi-coordinated submission.

In the meantime, I confessed to one of my confidantes that I would do my best to not listen to certain music (i.e., John Mayer) or actively follow Nineteen on social media. That's all I'd been doing since he broke up with me.

Ironically enough, throughout our relationship, Nineteen repeated how he rarely shared music with significant others because it could ruin it in the future. Although I can't speak for Nineteen, John Mayer isn't ruined for me. However, I certainly can't listen to him croon the lines from "Half of My Heart" without feeling like it's Nineteen's bittersweet love letter to me. I'd be amazed if he could listen to this album, let alone that song, without thinking of me, too.

It's no surprise I lost my appetite in the immediate aftermath of our ending. When I become deeply sad, the last thing I can do is eat. Nothing tastes good. Booze? Now that's no problem. Perhaps that's part of the reason I found myself sitting at a bar at 11:30 in the morning the following day, taking a "sick day" from work, drinking effervescent rosé next to a coconut latte while writing this. I could probably write a diet book, actually. I already have some solid marketing ideas – *Better than Atkins, better than Keto! Just have your heart broken and lose ten pounds in no time*! What would that one be called? *Diet Write*?

My therapist likened our tragic weekend to a "John Steinbeck novel." My mind immediately went to the desperation of the characters Steinbeck often portrayed. Which character was I? I didn't want to go that far for fear that I wouldn't like the answer. Her analogy was spot on, though.

"I'm waiting for him right now," I confessed to her.

Waiting for someone? Who was I? *Who had I become*? What did this mean, and did I know how long I was willing to wait? What were the logistics of waiting? Would I just know when enough was enough? *Ugh*, I didn't like this. As an innately impatient being, I've never liked waiting for anything, let alone any*one*.

I tried finding the silver lining. I began considering that I needed to know this pain, that I needed to have this experience. Was there comfort in that? Maybe. I later considered the very real possibility that maybe *he* needed to have this experience, and it didn't really have much to do with me at all. I did find comfort in that.

Even work couldn't keep me from texting Nineteen a few days after things ended:

Thinking about you and I hope you're doing well.

I was "still talking" to him. His half-assed response came an hour later:

Hey, I'm good thanks, busy like usual. Hope you're doing well too.

He used the b-word. I shook my head in familiar disappointment, and I never responded. And I stopped waiting. I wasn't going to see him again or "still talk" to him.

Today, I wonder if those two-plus hours of torturous road trip were Nineteen's opportunity to figure out what to say to spinelessly appease me, to avoid facing my tears. When he said that we should still talk, I truly believed I would hear from him, that goodbyes were unnecessary. Maybe that was my mistake. Or maybe he intended to "still talk" to me but never figured out what to do or say.

It was Bob Marley who once said, "The biggest coward is a man who awakens a woman's love without the intention of loving her." Some people will always be afraid of the deep end, never quite learning how to swim. If I'd known that Nineteen's words, "I think we should still talk," were more of conciliation than the truth, I would have mustered up every ounce of courage I had in my heart to say goodbye. I would have wanted a proper departure even amid my fear of goodbyes and deep sadness, but I suppose these words that you're reading will have to serve as the closure I think I still need. I think we both deserve that - even the coward.

THE MELTDOWN

"Well, are you gonna get back online and go for twenty?"

This question inevitably ensued after Nineteen was out of the picture.

While I'm a mildly competitive person, and I always do what I say I'm going to do, the resounding answer was, "No!" I didn't want to. I had no desire to even try because I believed that no one would come remotely close to my connection with Nineteen. So how could I bring myself to get back on the dating apps? How could I bring myself to go on a date with another stranger? *And for what*? To complete the challenge, to prove to myself, to you, and to Nineteen, what I already know?

I knew that online date number twenty would be a fill-in, a whatever, a what's-the-point, a rebound who might pull my pants down around my ankles and then be kicked out the door. That wouldn't be fair to either party involved. I'm not sure if my non-desire to go for twenty had more to do with the fact that Nineteen took an even greater toll on me than the eighteen that came before him or the fact that I was exhausted. It was probably a combination.

So, I did the next best thing I could think of because I was of complete sound mind and not feeling impulsive at all. I asked my gynecologist during a cervical biopsy in which she was concerned I might have cancer if she could reverse my tubal ligation. The answer she gave me was not what I was looking for. She said there was a high level of risk involved, and the chances of me ever becoming pregnant were slim. My best bet, should I ever decide I want children was, without a doubt, in vitro fertilization.

Not to mention that I might have cancer, so why would I even be thinking about having children anyhow (My thoughts, not my doctor's words). Thank God for my close friend who supportively came to the exam with me. She was cracking jokes about all the Botox she'd had, even managing to crack a smile upon my usually stoic doctor's face.

I'm not sure what I was thinking. However, if I were to take an honest stab at a guess, it probably had something to do with believing I'm never going to find someone to spend my life with so I might as well make a life that was stuck with me. Dumb and dumber, I know, and totally against everything I believe in, but as long as I was going back on the things I believe, why not go back on that, too? Also, dating Mr. Baby Crazy and then Nineteen made me dread meeting and falling for another man who wanted a family. Thankfully, no innocent lives were negatively affected during this not-so sound, deeply impetuous moment in my life.

Creativity and motivation are frequently spurred by pain, at least where I'm concerned. When motivation is present, good material is sure to rear its head. I bet if we surveyed a handful of songwriters, the majority of them would tell you that some of their best material came from loss or some form of sadness. Where else would all of the great love and breakup songs come from? *All by myself, don't wanna be all by...*Right, Eric Carmen?

I can hear everyone now: maybe Nineteen had to break your heart so you could finish your book. This seemed similar to the thought that Mr. Baby Crazy had to break my heart to begin the book.

Don't think I haven't had those painful thoughts. I'd just much rather be sitting here driven by the bliss of my relationship still going strong than telling you a sad story of loss. I don't care how entertaining it is.

The funny thing is, Nineteen was motivation even before he broke my heart. He was one of my biggest cheerleaders without even trying, his encouragement effortless. Even after being told he was "Nineteen" in a book about twenty online dates with twenty different men, this guy offered his own experiences and advice. If that's not something to be grateful for, I don't know what is.

If you recall, in telling Nineteen the synopsis of my book, I purposely left out the part about not wanting to make it to twenty. I did this because it felt like that was kind of the understood "you," in our case. The hopeless romantic in me likes to believe that words aren't always necessary when you share that kind of connection. I wanted Nineteen to be the "happy ending."

#*Spoileralert*: Nineteen is not the happy ending.

What it really boiled down to as I neared the end of the challenge my hairdresser assigned me was that I realized I could end this book any way I saw fit, in any way that served my wellbeing.

One night, while cheering on the Dodgers in the playoffs at my local bar, the same bar I'd taken three different online dates to, my friend Tila said, "We just gotta go through the duds to get to the stud."

Holy shit, she was right! I loved a good rhyme, and this one was hilariously accurate. Even the handsome stranger sitting near us, with the dog that kept trying to sniff my crotch, let out a discreet chuckle.

"That's going in my book!" I declared with a high five to the sky.

"Do you really feel like you need to be with someone right now?" Another friend questioned.

"I don't need anyone. I *want* someone."

And I knew the difference. I've never had a problem with being alone so much as a problem with the prospect of *always* being alone, of living alone. I realized everyone around me had that one person who would care if they passed. That person would be the one to make the call to the morgue at 4:30 in the morning to come to fetch their lifeless body from the room they once called theirs, where countless memories went to sleep before them. I was that person for my mama, and I wanted someone to be that person for me.

My brother has his wife and five children. My cousins have their families and significant others, and my favorite aunt has her immediate family. I'd since been deemed "The Adventurer" in the family, which on the surface sounds completely innocent and probably is. Unfortunately, for me, it holds negative connotations like the orphaned, abandoned magical, black sheep-unicorn hybrid of the family has spread her wings. These are my words, of course.

People always tell me how proud my mother would be of me and everything I've accomplished in life thus far. It often leaves me wondering if my mother were still around, would I have adventured so far? The simple answer to the question is *no*. The complex answer is *probably not*, but I'm grateful that I have. That answer can instill uncomfortable feelings of guilt.

Shortly after Nineteen and I ended, my brother from another mother, Jimmy, arrived in town for the weekend. He'd agreed to do a recording with me. He and I wrote, performed, and recorded music together for years. His being in town meant we got to spend some quality time catching up and commiserating on life. We'd planned to record a cover of the Jessie Ware song Nineteen showed me during our memorable evening after dining at Hey 19. It was the same song he requested I cover should I ever record music again.

"Equipment gets in the way of creativity," Jimmy said while we set up his small studio in prep for the recording.

We were tripping over wires and carrying hefty amps across the room. I couldn't help but feel like this applied to life and how the modern world connects. What if apps, technology, smartphones, etc., are getting in the way of the creativity of the natural connection, the natural order of things? What if the sparks caused by authentic connections weren't happening because there was so much excess, wires crossed, swipes made, constant disruption, and overstimulation?

After the day of the recording, it was exactly one week after Nineteen called it quits. It was also a year after losing the shorthaired loves of my life. In addition, I was getting my first tattoo, an imprint of my baby cat's paw right next to the permanent keloid scars from my oldest cat's claws. It felt like the right way to commemorate them, sort of the way recording a song that Nineteen wanted me to "one day" cover felt like the right way to grieve a relationship gone awry.

My phone lit up with a text message:

Have you talked to (insert Nineteen's two-syllable name here)?

It was James. The visual of Nineteen's name across my smartphone screen stung worse than the needle injecting black ink into my left forearm.

I haven't heard from him, no.

I really hope he gets some sense knocked into him, realizes what a great catch you are!

James made me feel better with his sentiment. It felt good being validated by another male. A week prior, I was sitting on a beach in Santa Barbara with Nineteen drinking a bottle of wine and people watching. I'd planned on asking him to join me at the tattoo session since he and I'd talked extensively about tattoos.

That night, I posted an Instagram photo of my tattoo, a black and grey replica of the cast of my baby George's left paw imprint.

Nineteen "liked" it.

While in therapy the following Wednesday evening, I had a total and unexpected meltdown. It was the ultimate meltdown of meltdowns. Parts of my face, particularly my lips and hands, went completely numb. My therapist said it was shock. I was just glad that the shock was happening on the couch my ass found so comfortable twice a week and not on my bedroom floor or in the driver's seat of my car during rush hour.

"I think I've been spending too much time shoving it all down and avoiding rather than allowing it to come out and feel it," I told her.

My meltdown was evident of my instinct. It was everything I was holding in while driving southbound on the 101 in the passenger seat of Nineteen's vehicle. It was listening to John Mayer's *Battle Studies* album on repeat. It was Nineteen's "I can't do this anymore." It was his, "I think we should still talk," and it was losing my cats. It was missing my mother and being abandoned by my brother. It was all the feelings I'd been shoving down to make someone else more comfortable for the last few months. No matter how often I'm taught to take care of myself first, I always put others' feelings ahead of mine, especially if I care a lot about said person. It was *everybody leaving*. It was even about my dad.

I don't know if it's easier to be angry with the dead or easier to be sad, but I know that sadness makes more sense the more I learn and the longer I live. My dad did the best he could. He was human just like me and the rest of the characters you've been reading about – even Mr. Baby Crazy and, dare I say it, even David, my ex-husband. It's difficult to be angry with someone who did the best he could with what he'd learned from the people who did the best they could and so forth. It's a lot easier to acknowledge that we are all human, and we learn from our experiences and those who raise us. It's a lot easier to be saddened by the fact that my father's relief came in the form of harmful substances. It made more sense to be sad rather than angry that I never had the kind of relationship I craved and deserved from the first man I ever knew.

My meltdown was par for the course, and I'd been there before. I had nowhere to direct the overflowing reservoir of love that had developed over the course of my lifetime. I had yet to ever meet someone capable of receiving the kind of love I have to offer. The saddest part of it all was that I was aware I lived in a world where one of the most remarkable connections I've ever had with someone still existed. He was out there, living and breathing just as I was, though I was struggling for breath in between the uncontrollable sobs. This made no sense to my idealist mind and passionate heart. No matter how hard I try to make sense out of it today, at times, I still have difficulty grasping the logic. It was proof that holding things inside does no one any good. Mr. Baby Crazy could learn a lesson or two in that area, but he was too busy projecting his fears upon framed skeletal art printed on dictionary paper in his former girlfriend's bedroom.

Nineteen stopped following me on Instagram somewhere between my receiving an email from Coffee Meets Bagel that my personal information may have been compromised and my attempt at filling up my schedule with something to drink, I mean *do*. I learned the details surrounding the dating app's security breach while wallowing in my grief over a bottle of red wine. Nineteen and I would not "still talk" after all, not even in the superficial arena of social media.

During my hiatus from Coffee Meets Bagel, I received another email claiming that I was in the top 30% of the "most liked people" on their app. They probably sent that email to all of their inactive accounts, I thought. And mine had been inactive since my third date with Nineteen, the one where he'd asked me to be his plus one for his aunt's eightieth. I rolled my eyes, scrolling to the fine print at the bottom, searching for the link to unsubscribe from the bullshit.

My weekends were full of activities. I was deliberately *busy* but not dating. I've always believed that everyone we meet has a purpose, even if that person only exchanges a friendly glance or a cordial hello with us. What did they add to my life at that moment? How did they make me feel? What did they make me think of? Somewhere around Nineteen, I began asking what *I* added to his life? How did I make him feel? What thoughts did I conjure up in his mind? I like to think that he thinks of me every time he sees or uses his Bridlewood wine opener.

It was a Sunday afternoon when one of my best friends, Sandy, and I were immersed in some day drinking. I told Sandy how my mother always taught me that the price of love is grief. There was certainly no greater lesson in that adage than after she died. The bartender, overhearing our forlorn conversation in which I began divulging details of the moment Nineteen broke my heart, shared his feelings on the matter of love.

"I'm in love with being in love. *So in love*, in fact, that I'd swim a river just to get to the next time."

This wasn't someone who'd never been hurt, either. He went on to explain that no matter how poorly a relationship may end, he'd never give up. I think we could all learn a little something about living life to the fullest from this man. Ready to swim a river, for God's sake! I'd be standing there asking how cold and clean the water is.

GOOD LUCK

My friend, James, with whom I'd exchanged many online dating stories, was disappointed to learn that my relationship didn't work out, first with Mr. Baby Crazy and then with Nineteen. One afternoon, he texted me:

Time for you to move on, away from all the man babies, to find someone strong enough for you.

I'm not holding my breath.

When he proposed getting together on a Saturday night, I figured there was no harm in laughing about our online dating experiences over cocktails. Was I still in a vulnerable place? Yes. Had James and I ever gone out just the two of us before? No. We were always in the company of mutual friends. I'd known James for years, though, and he was a good, honest, and respectable man. So, I checked my vulnerability the moment after I sent the text message, agreeing to meet up with him.

In the two days leading up to our outing, there was a lot more texting and what felt like borderline flirting. I wasn't averse to it, either. In fact, I was *enjoying* it. We challenged each other's livers with messages like, "Hope you can keep up." after deciding it best to both take an Uber to the downtown Los Angeles bar, El Dorado. It was a sexy, literal underground bar complete with hardwood floors, leather booths, and incredible mood lighting. It was retrofitted into the basement of a high rise listed on the National Registrar of Historic Buildings.

As soon as my Uber driver picked me up, she and I became instant friends. Thirty minutes later, as we arrived downtown, Mindi knew the nutshell details of what I was doing (going on what I *think* was a date), and with whom I was meeting with (a long-time friend), as well as the synopsis of the book I was writing (duh).

"I'm going to need a follow-up – I gotta know how this pans out!" She requested with unexpected enthusiasm.

"I'm kinda nervous," I admitted two blocks from the destination. I think my nerves were due to the fact that I wasn't sure if this was a date or just two people who've known each other for a long time meeting up to hang out.

Mindi offered some unsolicited, though welcomed, advice, "If you're nervous, you're focusing on yourself and the result, and the moment is not about you. If you focus on your intention and the result you want with the other person, you will find it easier to stay in the moment. You'll avoid feelings of anxiety and sabotage."

While that was a lot to take in, its gist helped to shift my focus. It made me realize James was probably feeling similarly. So, I stopped carrying all of the weight of those nerves spurred by fear as we pulled up to El Dorado.

I thanked her and said, "I know we just met, but I'd love to get your number." Imagine if meeting and getting to know someone was always that easy! Oh, wait, it is! We humans always manage to complicate the shit out of the simplest acts. Mindi and I exchanged numbers, and I had every intention of following through.

James was running slightly late, so I sipped a glass of rosé at the bar in the hopes of calming any residual anxiety while mulling over my Uber driver's sage advice. Okay, I'm lying – I downed a glass of rosé because even if the advice was well-received, it was also easier said than done. I opted for rosé because I didn't want to come away with red wine mouth.

I wore a fiery red blouse with big, gold hoop earrings, my wavy hair kissing my bare shoulders. I opted for camel-colored strappy heels but not too high. Even if this wasn't a date, I still wanted to dress the part. Better to be overdressed than underdressed.

The bar was empty aside from a lone patron enjoying his whiskey on the rocks and a couple cuddled near one another in a giant booth when my phone lit up with a text from James.

Just pulling up.

A couple minutes later, he came walking into the bar looking dressed for a date, as well: white, button-down shirt with a barely visible, black pinstripe, dark jeans, and a big smile he wore so well. And those dimples! How had I never noticed those dimples? I hopped off my stool to greet him, casually, of course. We hugged, and as we pulled apart, he handed me one long-stemmed, red rose. Yep, this was a date. If his attire didn't confirm the occasion, the thornless rose certainly did. I brought the velvety petals to my nose, inhaling its lovely aroma.

"Wow, thank you!" I was genuinely surprised at not only the gesture but at my own delight with it. I silently thought, *thank God it wasn't a dozen.*

We sat down, our knees casually grazing as the bartender greeted my company. James ordered a jack and coke, and I ordered my second rosé.

We laughed, and we flirted, occasionally reaching out to touch one another's arms. Maybe Mr. Baby Crazy was right? I should be with the "tall, dark, and handsome man with tattoos." I had, in fact, spent more time with James and known him longer than any of the previously mentioned potential mates.

It didn't take long into our conversation that scarcely revolved around others we'd dated to confess our mutual attraction. Did it seem soon? Yes. Was I going to shy away from its potential because

Nineteen had let me go weeks prior? No. James knew the facts, and he wasn't shying away, either.

"I've been attracted to you for quite some time but didn't want to jeopardize our friendship," James confessed.

"The feeling is mutual, but what's changed that made you decide to take that risk now?" I asked.

"Well, I figured the possibility of there being something between us is greater than the risk. Plus, we're both adults and friends, first."

As I silently weighed the risk, a growing crowd began closing in around us. We decided to grab a bite to eat. It was already pretty late, close to 1 a.m. by the time we pushed our way through the Saturday night drunkards and left.

Guisados, one of my favorite taco spots, was within walking distance. Over a couple of shrimp tacos and more uninterrupted conversation, my mind was racing. What was happening? *Was I really on a date with James*? The reality of the situation began settling in with the sobriety.

"I can't believe I'm sitting across from James (*insert his sexy last name here*) at almost 2 a.m., on a Saturday night."

He returned the sentiment just before feeling something hit the back of his neck. Reaching back with his napkin, he revealed a black, oily-looking residue. I looked up to see a fat pigeon perched directly above him.

"That bird just shit on your head!" I couldn't suppress the hilarity, cracking up at James' presumed misfortune.

"Ugh!" James looked around for the nearest restroom.

"That's good luck, ya know!" He'd never heard of this, but I took it as a sign. "Better you than me!" I added as he walked away.

After my favorite food and pigeon poop (that just sounds disgusting in the same sentence), we wandered arm in arm. All of the bars were closing, and the drunks were beginning to walk the streets of downtown LA. It felt surprisingly comfortable to be in this close physical proximity with James, our bodies moving seamlessly together like we'd been doing this for quite some time.

He tugged at my hand, motioning for me to follow him to a concrete wall on the corner of 5th and Olive in Pershing Square, the historic Millennium Biltmore hotel as the backdrop. I sat on the wall, eye-level with James' chest. I looked up into his eyes, and we smiled timidly. Both buzzed and giddy from all of the unexpected feelings that present themselves during great first dates, he went in for the first kiss. It was wonderful, better than I imagined because yes, I'd imagined it.

Coming up for air, I boldly asked, "Would you like to come home with me?"

His eyes lit up like the high-rise buildings behind him, and those goddamned dimples revealed themselves again. Of course, he wanted to come home with me. Asking him to go home with me was a valid exception to my first date rule because *I knew him*. He was a friend, a familiar face, someone who'd *known me* for years. Not to mention, it just felt right.

We Ubered back to my place, where we plopped ourselves down on my living room floor and smoked a joint together. We listened to and shared music. I played Miguel's "Simple Things," hoping he'd pick up what I was putting down, and he did, shortly before putting down something of his own.

"I wanna be number twenty," he professed.

I giggled. "You're just high. Besides, it doesn't count 'cause we didn't meet online..." I paused. "*But*, I can end my book any way I want."

One thing led to another, and I was face down, ass up in the wee hours of a Sunday morning with a man whom I'd called a good friend for almost six years. We woke up naked next to one another and spent the next three hours talking and doing yoga in my bedroom before grabbing breakfast at a nearby diner.

"I can't believe I woke up with James (*insert his sexy last name again here*) and am now having breakfast with him."

"I can't believe I was doing yoga stretches on Lindsay Dellinger's bedroom floor this morning, in my underwear." He countered.

As I drove him home after breakfast, I worried that we'd crossed a line. What if that was it? What if that was the last time I'd wake up to James in my bed and the last time I'd have breakfast with him? The hug we gave each other as we bid our see-you-laters eased those worries.

Our second date involved cheering on the Los Angeles Dodgers at a Burbank bar. It became very clear very quickly how if something had the potential to last, it wasn't going to feel like hard work. All relationships are work, but I think I'd convinced myself that if I worked hard and gave something subpar every ounce of my emotional energy, then it would all be worth it in the end. It took falling for a friend to realize that it didn't have to feel like work at all. Maybe there's some truth to that idea that love is right underneath our noses. We only need to stop "looking" for it?

About a month after the John Steinbeck novel of a weekend, I took my first solo trip up to Santa Ynez to fetch my wine club bottles from Bridlewood. The plan was to get in some productive writing, as well. En route, I saw it - The emerald green roof next to the Airbnb I'd rented for a weekend getaway perched atop a hill in Summerland overlooking the Pacific Ocean. It was the structure Nineteen asked if I could see as we drove toward our dramatic demise. The blue, fall sky served as a refreshing framework to the bittersweet setting. I stopped in Summerland because I had an hour to kill before the winery opened.

The man selling goods at the corner liquor store, the very one where Nineteen had fetched us water, greeted me as if he knew me.

He assisted me in finding a pen for purchase, even writing with it to ensure it worked before bidding me a "see you again, soon." Did he know something I didn't? Had he seen something I hadn't? It wouldn't be the first time mystics took a bow in this life I've been living.

I sat on a bench outside Red Kettle Coffee, sipping on the familiar taste of coconut latte. I was writing with my new pen, wondering what a simple life would feel like living, where every weekend was friendly faces of strangers you never quite get to know past a "good morning" smile and golden hour strolls down quiet, sleepy streets with your ride or die. I wondered what this simple life would have been like with Nineteen, recalling a conversation we'd once had about that mutual daydream, its boundaries not limited to North America. This daydream was fleeting as the memory that he'd been reduced to one of the strangers came to fruition.

Later that afternoon, while wine tasting at a small winery in Los Olivos, my phone lit up with a text message from a number I didn't recognize:

How have you been?

Hi! I'm so sorry - Who is this?

(Insert The Doctor's full name, AKA first online date ever, AKA guy who likes to suck on toes). It's been a long time. Was just going through my phone.

Oh, wow…so sorry. I hadn't heard from you in so long. I am well. How are you?

No worries. I realize it's been forever. I'm doing well. What have you been up to?

I am currently wine tasting/writing solo up on the central coast this weekend? What have you been up to?

Oh nice. Enjoy! Just been working a lot. Need more balance in my life haha. E.g. wine haha

Haha Thanks…honestly, did not think I'd ever be hearing from you again.

Likewise. Didn't really hear from you when you came back from Japan.

Seemed like you'd moved on, like you weren't looking for anything too serious at the time so I stopped reaching out. What the hell made you reach out after all this time?

Honestly was just going through my phone and cleaning my phone book. Figured I'd reach out.

Well, it's nice to hear from you. What r u up to this wknd?

I just need to relax this weekend haha

I wasn't about to bite on his need to relax. That bait was dried up and unappetizing, albeit entertaining. I never responded, and he hopefully "cleaned out" my number from his phone because I clearly *cleaned* him out of mine.

During the weekend, when I wasn't busily typing away on my laptop, James and I were sharing pictures, songs, texting, flirting, and checking in with one another.

Hey you! Just thinking about you and hope you're having a wonderful day so far. It's so fucking beautiful here – perfect weather. I discovered a new winery only a lil over an hour outside LA. I will definitely be returning in the near future – hopefully with you.

Hey, you were on my mind…you're having a wonderful day relaxing. I can picture you smiling. Would totally join you the next time you head out there.

As I crawled into bed at my Airbnb that night, James sent me an image describing a *soulmate* along with this text:

It's a great feeling how much we exchange…the laughs and how we express how we feel about each other. I came across this and this describes it all!! You have more than just my attention (*insert kissy face emoji*).

Wow...do you really feel that way? That's heavy and beautiful. Like I told you last night, I woke up one morning and my whole life had changed again. You have been a part of my life for the last six years but you're a different and more important part of it now and it feels so easy and so good.

There's a connection that we've been sharing and it's deeper than just going out on a date and separate from the kisses and hugs we exchange. You truly make me happy and I'm constantly thinking about you/us. It was meant for us to take our time to get to know each other through friendship. Answer to your question – Yesss that's how I really feel!! (*Insert two monkeys covering their eyes emojis*).

You're fucking awesome. I appreciate your honesty and integrity more than you may know.

We spent the three-day weekend after Thanksgiving together in Ojai. During that time, I had the opportunity to share my self-proclaimed happy place with him, California's central coast wine country, and Bridlewood. James was never much of a wine drinker, but he quickly became one after spending so much time with me. Even better, he enjoyed it. After becoming inspired, he decided to use his artistic skill and passion to do wine-inspired paintings.

James and I'd reached "good morning, handsome" meme status by this time, which quickly turned into more risqué quotes of the day about our most primal desires for each other.

In the form of a meme, I sent him:

Date someone you can have rough sex and deep conversations with whether it's at two in the morning or two in the afternoon.

He replied with an image of his own that read:

Find someone whose demons are compatible with yours. (*Insert smiling devil emoji*)

We got each other. I was so excited that I'd finally met someone who didn't shy away from telling me what he wanted and enjoyed it when I told him what I wanted. I could be naughty, and I could be sweet, and James would receive it all. There was active, mutual participation, appreciation, and, most importantly, communication.

We spent every other weekend together and some school nights. I'd unexpectedly receive poems he'd write about us in the middle of the afternoon, complete with graphic descriptions, sexual, fantastical, and otherwise. Time seemed to fly by. It was full of delicious date nights, Miguel's music, and Sundays where we'd both just paint and write in the company of one another when we weren't exploring eachother's bodies underneath soft, bamboo cotton sheets. It felt as if I was right where I belonged.

MY RIDE OR DIE

Alongside the incredible feelings that this relationship was conjuring up, the familiar feeling that it was too good to be true weighed heavy. I was constantly waiting for the other shoe to drop. Nothing and no man could be this good. I've learned that my "safe" place is the place where I'm consistently disappointed. As long as I can count on this, I'll always be in control. Programmed to believe I couldn't possibly be good enough for a man who wouldn't disappoint me, I grappled with feeling like I'm worthy of the kind of love I idealize.

Unlearning things and truths I was taught, and I've told myself my whole life, has been one of the hardest things I've ever done. It's a daily struggle to be true to myself, be honest with myself, and hold myself accountable. It's an ongoing struggle getting to the point where, one day, my heart and my mind will agree and coexist, where I'll always be enough. Unfortunately, no app on Earth could ever come close to easing those insecurities. To "break the pattern," I had to play Mortal Kombat with my fears.

I spoke to James in great lengths about these fears and my dark.

"I'm not going anywhere. It doesn't scare me." He calmly assures me.

While this is that unfamiliarity I speak of that frightens me, I also know it's exactly what I've been looking for, craved, needed, and deserved my whole life.

While James is one of the easiest people to be vulnerable with, thirty-plus years of existence will still shout in my ear, "Be careful! He might disappoint you like everyone else, or he might leave…like everyone else."

I'm fighting every inclination and fear to not push him away. He's aware of my tendency to push away the bliss that is entirely foreign to me. Even through my anger, confusion, and projections, he's still here, one of the most patient men I've ever met.

Over our first holidays together, we spent five days straight with one another, on the road, testing that patience. From a hotel room in Monterey to an Airbnb in the middle of the redwood forest and a townhome in Mammoth, we feasted on the best seafood, rode a roller coaster, and laughed our butts off in a deep soaking clawfoot tub after eating cannabis-infused chocolate on Christmas night.

"Slow down! A gnome might jump out and surprise you." I'd joke, and we'd laugh as he sped down winding one-lane roads framed in soaring, stunning redwoods. The setting was pleasantly eerie, with lush green leaves and gnarly branches almost scraping the sunroof of his SUV. The thick fog lifted itself inches off a dewing forest floor as I oohed and aahed at the scenery while internally oohing and aahing at the progress of our relationship.

Once we got to the Mammoth area, I didn't have to tell him to "Slow down." The heavy snow falling as night crept in was enough to make everyone slow down. I navigated while he kept his eyes peeled to the slick road and his hands at ten and two on the wheel.

Our compatibility and strength as a team became more apparent than ever before once we made it to shelter. We conveyed how nervous and stressed we both were on that snowy highway without making it noticeable to the other. We maintained our composure to achieve a mutual goal, reach safety sans any added stress that could have stemmed from one or both of us freaking out.

If someone had asked if I saw James and me while sitting at the Miguel concert, desperately craving Nineteen's affection, I would have laughed at what would've sounded entirely too far-fetched for my heart at the time. If someone had told me that Mr. Baby Crazy's insecure thoughts weren't so crazy after all, I would have rolled my eyes. It's proof that nothing ever works out the way we foresee it or the way we think we need it to.

I still chat with Mr. East Coast from time to time. Most recently, he texted me:

Hi LindsAy. Thinking of you.

It happened to be a particularly rough day, so it was a welcomed sentiment to be thought of by him. I think we'll always care about each other due in large part to how similar we are. Keeping him in my orbit no longer has anything to do with the possibility of romance and more to do with the human being he is and the connection we share. Most importantly, he knows about James and though I didn't go into great detail with him, I left it at how happy I am. He, in turn, expressed his happiness for me.

Mr. East Coast was a great introduction to the very clear difference between a man and a boy, an adult and a child, and, for that, I'm grateful. A boy will make you believe he wants a commitment until shit becomes real. A man will tell you exactly what he's looking for and/or what he's capable of.

The night I realized I was so similar to many of the unavailable men I'd found myself in an intimate relationship with was a very emotional night. It was my first Valentine's Day with James. Through tears and anxiety, I admitted to him that I, too, had built walls that I didn't really know existed until that moment. Would I learn how to manage my walls before I destroyed the beauty of a friendship that had developed into something deeper? When Nineteen relayed his walls to me, why couldn't I acknowledge my own, and what difference would it have made? So many questions and so few answers were threatening to open a wound that hadn't quite healed.

This would have been my truth, whether I had been challenged to online date or not. Technology may change the process, but we're still participating in a relationship that requires human-to-human contact at the end of the day. After that initial swipe right, one must get out from behind the cell phone screen and conduct themselves in a functioning society full of human interaction. It may begin with technology, but it will not end with it. Regardless of technological developments, dating apps can't lighten our proverbial baggage.

*

Our "I can't believe I'm with Lindsay/James" doing this or that sentiment happened often during our courtship. It happened the first time we went grocery shopping together and the first time I stayed the night at his place. It happened the first time he went wine tasting and the first time I watched *The Thomas Crown Affair*. It happened during the most mundane of moments and the most significant, and it still happens from time to time.

I was looking for that good man my mother didn't believe existed because, against all odds, I continued believing he did exist. I was looking for what I told Nineteen I was looking for on our first date – my ride or die. I was looking for that man who will choose me every damned time, who is not going to leave or shy away from my dark, and whom I'm not going to leave out of my fear of the unfamiliar. James is that man. We are each other's ride or die right now, and right now is all any of us have.

Did you know in some cultures, superstition states that you're more likely to win the lottery than to be pooped on by a bird? This is why it's considered good luck. I kinda feel like that pigeon shit on my head, too.

ACKNOWLEDGEMENTS

First and foremost, I'd like to thank Coffee Meets Bagel and Bumble, for if it weren't for modern dating apps, this book wouldn't have been possible. A huge shoutout to my editors, Amanda Gersh and Kasey Herrin, for lending their eyes, ears, experiences, time, and reading/writing expertise to this body of work. I'd probably be somewhere around draft 2 if it weren't for you two. *Thank you*. Thank you to the many men in this story. If some of you hadn't swiped right, I'd have nothing to write. Thank you to John Mayer, Miguel, and Sigur Rós – your beautiful melodies and relatable lyrics provided an endless soundtrack for many late nights of wining and writing, as well as an audible element to the contents of this memoir. Thank you to Charles Bukowski and the dozens of writers before me for elegantly putting into words some of the human complexities expressed in this memoir. Thank you to the many friends and family members who endured hours of online dating shenanigan stories. Thank you for always responding to my text messages about what I was wearing, where I was going to be, and who I was going to be with. Thank you to my love for always encouraging and supporting my writing, being the most patient man I know, and for contributing your graphic design skills. Lastly, but certainly not least, thank *YOU*, the reader. Thank you for reading my story – I do hope you've enjoyed the ride.

ACKNOWLEDGMENTS

Lindsay Taylor Dellinger is a former fashion industry Art Director/Graphic Artist. She currently writes for various publications and freelance designs. *Swipe Write* is her debut memoir, and she maintains a blog, www.TheRoadLindsTravels.com, covering everything from her travels to her love for wine. She and her partner bought a school bus in March of 2021. They have since been converting it (DIY-style) into a tiny home on wheels with the intent of living an alternative lifestyle and traveling full time. Their adopted senior feline, Sir Benson Brunello, The First & Only (Benson, for short), makes three. Lindsay calls Los Angeles, California home.

www.Lindsay-Taylor-Dellinger.com
Facebook.com/TheRoadLindsTravels
Instagram: @The_Road_Linds_Travels
Twitter: @Leend_Sigh

Made in the USA
Middletown, DE
01 April 2023

27388998R00186